New Daylight

Edited by **Sally Welch**   September–December 2018

The Bible Reading Fellowship
15 The Chambers, Vineyard
Abingdon OX14 3FE
brf.org.uk

The Bible Reading Fellowship (BRF) is a Registered Charity (233280)

ISBN 978 0 85746 599 3

This edition © The Bible Reading Fellowship 2018
Cover image and illustration on page 141 © Thinkstock

Distributed in Australia by:
MediaCom Education Inc, PO Box 610, Unley, SA 5061
Tel: 1 800 811 311 | admin@mediacom.org.au

Distributed in New Zealand by:
Scripture Union Wholesale, PO Box 760, Wellington
Tel: 04 385 0421 | suwholesale@clear.net.nz

Acknowledgements
Scripture quotations marked GNT are from: Good News Translation® (Today's English Version, Second Edition). Copyright © 1992 American Bible Society. All rights reserved.

KJV: the Authorised Version of the Bible (The King James Bible), the rights in which are vested in the Crown, reproduced by permission of the Crown's Patentee, Cambridge University Press.

MSG: *The Message*, copyright © 1993, 1994, 1995, 1996, 2000, 2001, 2002 by Eugene H. Peterson. Used by permission of NavPress. All rights reserved. Represented by Tyndale House Publishers, Inc.

NIRV: The Holy Bible, New International Reader's Version. Copyright © 1996, 1998 Biblica. All rights reserved throughout the world. Used by permission of Biblica. New International Reader's Version and NIrV are registered trademarks of Biblica.

NIV: The Holy Bible, New International Version, Anglicised edition, copyright © 1979, 1984, 2011 by Biblica. Used by permission of Hodder & Stoughton Publishers, an Hachette UK company. All rights reserved. 'NIV' is a registered trademark of Biblica. UK trademark number 1448790.

NLT: The Holy Bible, New Living Translation, copyright © 1996, 2004, 2007, 2013. Used by permission of Tyndale House Publishers, Inc., Carol Stream, Illinois 60188. All rights reserved.

NRSV: The New Revised Standard Version of the Bible, Anglicised Edition, copyright © 1989, 1995 by the Division of Christian Education of the National Council of the Churches of Christ in the USA. Used by permission. All rights reserved.

TLB: The Living Bible copyright © 1971 by Tyndale House Foundation. Used by permission of Tyndale House Publishers Inc., Carol Stream, Illinois 60188. All rights reserved. The Living Bible, TLB, and the The Living Bible logo are registered trademarks of Tyndale House Publishers.

Printed by Gutenberg Press, Tarxien, Malta

Suggestions for using New Daylight

Find a regular time and place, if possible, where you can read and pray undisturbed. Before you begin, take time to be still and perhaps use the BRF Prayer on page 6. Then read the Bible passage slowly (try reading it aloud if you find it over-familiar), followed by the comment. You can also use *New Daylight* for group study and discussion, if you prefer.

The prayer or point for reflection can be a starting point for your own meditation and prayer. Many people like to keep a journal to record their thoughts about a Bible passage and items for prayer. In *New Daylight* we also note the Sundays and some special festivals from the church calendar, to keep in step with the Christian year.

New Daylight and the Bible

New Daylight contributors use a range of Bible versions, and you will find a list of the versions used opposite. You are welcome to use your own preferred version alongside the passage printed in the notes. This can be particularly helpful if the Bible text has been abridged.

New Daylight affirms that the whole of the Bible is God's revelation to us, and we should read, reflect on and learn from every part of both Old and New Testaments. Usually the printed comment presents a straightforward 'thought for the day', but sometimes it may also raise questions rather than simply providing answers, as we wrestle with some of the more difficult passages of Scripture.

New Daylight is also available in a deluxe edition (larger format). Visit your local Christian bookshop or contact the BRF office, who can also give details about a cassette version for the visually impaired. For a Braille edition, contact St John's Guild, Sovereign House, 12–14 Warwick Street, Coventry CV5 6ET.

Comment on New Daylight

To send feedback, please email **enquiries@brf.org.uk**, phone **+44 (0)1865 319700** or write to the address shown opposite.

Writers in this issue

Amanda Bloor is a parish priest on the Isle of Wight, a director of ordinands and a chaplain to a variety of youth and community organisations. She loves engaging with people's questions about faith and encouraging individuals to follow God's calling. In her spare time she enjoys walks on the beach, making music with others and reading voraciously.

Amy Boucher Pye is the author of *The Living Cross: Exploring God's gift of forgiveness and new life* (BRF, 2016) and the award-winning *Finding Myself in Britain* (Authentic Media, 2015). She enjoys running the *Woman Alive* book club and speaking at churches. She blogs at **amyboucherpye.com**.

Debbie Orriss has been in Christian ministry as a Church Army evangelist for over 20 years. She is currently Discipleship Coordinator for Salisbury Diocese, and is passionate about helping children and adults discover that God loves them to bits and invites them into life in all its fullness.

Stephen Rand is an activist, a writer and a speaker who worked with Tearfund and Open Doors, travelling widely. He is now responsible for the public communications of the All-Party Parliamentary Group on International Freedom of Religion or Belief.

Nick Read, a fellow of the Royal Agricultural Society, is director of the Bulmer Foundation, a sustainable development charity based in Hereford. He is also a volunteer agricultural chaplain with Borderlands Rural Chaplaincy, an ecumenical chaplaincy covering the English–Welsh Marches.

Fiona Stratta is a speech and language therapist, a speech and drama teacher, and the author of *Walking with Gospel Women* (BRF, 2012), *Walking with Old Testament Women* (BRF, 2015) and *Walking with Biblical Women of Courage* (BRF, 2017). In her writings she desires to connect readers' spiritual journeys more closely to their daily lives.

Penelope Wilcock writes Christian fiction, pastoral theology and Bible study. Her books include *Spiritual Care of Dying and Bereaved People* (BRF, 2013). She blogs at **kindredofthequietway.blogspot.co.uk**.

David Winter is retired from parish ministry. An honorary Canon of Christ Church, Oxford, he is well known as a writer and broadcaster. His most recent book for BRF is *Heaven's Morning: Rethinking our destination*.

Sally Welch writes...

As we enter autumn and winter it is tempting to become mournful, sighing for the relaxed greenness of summer months, looking back to the vivid hope of spring. Such reflections can be useful, in that it is in pondering that we learn 'emotion recollected in tranquillity', as Wordsworth describes it. Indeed, one of the key characteristics of Mary, whose nature is explored by Penelope Wilcock in this issue, is the way she holds the events of Jesus' life in her heart and ponders them. Joshua too makes remembering an important part of his leadership, and Fiona Stratta shows Joshua's skill in encouraging the children of Israel to recall God's goodness to them in the past in order to inspire them to live well and faithfully into the future. Nick Read explores the challenging book of Leviticus, with its seemingly endless descriptions of the best way to sacrifice an animal, and shows how adherence to the covenant which God made with this people is both honoured and replaced by Christ's sacrifice on the cross. He demonstrates how a willingness to grapple with Leviticus will help Christians understand the context in which Christ lived and the eternal truths which he brought to fruition.

However, to dwell too long amid memories can sap one's energies for engaging with the present and looking to the future, preventing new growth and progress. Amy Boucher Pye shows us how accepting the forgiveness of Christ for ourselves is as necessary for living fully in Christ as engaging with the challenging task of forgiving others.

This process of forgiveness is just as important in public life as in the domestic sphere. As the nations of the world unite in remembering and mourning the loss of so many lives in the tragedy of World War I at the centenary of its ending, we join our prayers with those of Christians throughout the world as we pledge to work for peace on a worldwide scale. The scarlet poppy, a powerful symbol of blood spilt, is also a sign of new growth and hope for the future: 'To you from failing hands we throw the torch; be yours to hold it high' ('In Flanders Fields' by John McCrae).

As we journey through the autumn and winter months I pray that we may grow in the understanding and love from which spring the shoots of forgiveness.

Sally Ann Welch

The BRF Prayer

Almighty God,
you have taught us that your word is a lamp for our feet
and a light for our path. Help us, and all who prayerfully
read your word, to deepen our fellowship with you
and with each other through your love.
And in so doing may we come to know you more fully,
love you more truly, and follow more faithfully
in the steps of your son Jesus Christ, who lives and reigns
with you and the Holy Spirit, one God for evermore.
Amen

Colossians

The letter to the Colossians does not end with 'Yours faithfully' or 'Yours sincerely' – even though it came from a writer who was full of faith and very sincere. Instead it ends with 'I, Paul, write this greeting in my own hand. Remember my chains. Grace be with you' (4:18, NIV).

The apostle Paul was in prison. It seems that he may have dictated the letter, and then personally signed it off. Facing severe troubles of his own, nevertheless he was prompted to take the trouble to write to this group of Christians.

Why the Colossians? Who were they? Where were they? Located right in the centre of the Roman province of Asia Minor (what is now Turkey), Colossae had once been an important city, a place of commerce. A significant number of Jewish exiles from Babylon had been settled there around 200BC. But Colossae had fallen on hard times, and not long after this letter arrived, an earthquake effectively destroyed the city.

There's no mention in the book of Acts that Paul ever visited Colossae. But Epaphras, a close friend of Paul, came from the city. One theory is that Epaphras heard about Jesus from Paul in Ephesus, and took the good news back to his home town. That would explain why Paul felt a responsibility to write to this small group of Christians, to build and shape their faith. Perhaps Epaphras had reported to Paul that there were signs that they were struggling to differentiate between their faith in Christ and all the other religious and philosophical thinking swirling around them. So he got in touch.

I wonder if you can see any similarities here? Hopefully not that you feel insignificant and unvisited or that you might be getting hold of the wrong end of the stick! Rather, someone you have never met face-to-face, but who seems to know all about you and cares deeply about you, has made a great deal of effort to communicate with you.

The amazing thing is, the words that prisoner Paul wrote to that little church in Turkey 2,000 years ago are God's words to you today. My prayer is that you will hear, and be guided and encouraged.

STEPHEN RAND

Faith and love

Paul, an apostle of Christ Jesus by the will of God... To God's holy people in Colossae, the faithful brothers and sisters in Christ... We always thank God, the Father of our Lord Jesus Christ, when we pray for you, because we have heard of your faith in Christ Jesus and of the love you have for all God's people – the faith and love that spring from the hope stored up for you in heaven and about which you have already heard in the true message of the gospel that has come to you.

Paul begins by gently but firmly asserting the authority by which he writes. He is 'an apostle', a messenger, one who brings the word of God. But he emphasises that he is not self-appointed to this role, but rather chosen by God for it. His account of the dramatic encounter on the road to Damascus (see Acts 22:1–21) is testimony to that.

And just as his role and calling come from God, so too does the group of believers he writes to: 'God's holy people in Colossae'. They belong to God; they are 'in Christ'. They are more than just a disparate group of people who believe (roughly) the same things and get together once a week to sing songs of worship. They are 'brothers and sisters', part of God's family, bound together with 'cords that cannot be broken', as the old hymn 'Bind Us Together' says.

They certainly are given a wonderful endorsement. The cynic will think that Paul is buttering them up, ready for the good talking-to he wants to give them. But they would surely have been impressed by the good report that Epaphras had clearly given them: 'we have heard of your faith... and of the love you have...'

Faith in Jesus and love for people go together. If only more churches down through history had earned this same commendation! I am so grateful that in my work with Tearfund and Open Doors I have met so many who have combined faith and love in a dynamic people-changing and community-changing way.

'The true message of the gospel' is the one that prompts and provokes faith in God and love for others in an inseparable way of living.

STEPHEN RAND

Good news

In the same way, the gospel is bearing fruit and growing throughout the whole world – just as it has been doing among you since the day you heard it and truly understood God's grace.

When this letter was written, around 30 years after the death and resurrection of Jesus, there were no more than a few thousand people who would have described themselves as Christians. Yet Paul confidently writes that the gospel was growing throughout the whole world.

To many it would have seemed a vain boast or wishful thinking. But Paul has travelled the Roman world and seen people of every race and position in society willing to follow Jesus even when it meant persecution or martyrdom. He knows that God is at work – that an unstoppable movement has been unleashed in the power of the Holy Spirit.

It is still growing! I remember a colleague at Tearfund who as a young missionary in India had every year travelled to the borders of the Kingdom of Nepal, which was completely closed to the outside world, and prayed that one day those borders would open to the gospel. And now? The estimate is that there are nearly one million Nepali Christians.

In China the authorities did all they could to crush the church through years of brutal persecution. Now they are trying to control religion again, unnerved by the growth of a church that may have reached over 100 million people. Whoever living at the time of Chairman Mao would have guessed that 40 years later *The Times* would be reporting that by 2030 China could have the world's largest Christian population?

A third of the world's population now describe themselves as Christians. But true and meaningful growth has to include what Paul describes as 'bearing fruit'. It is not enough to claim the name of Christ; the gospel has to be lived out in loving compassion and witness. It flows from the head to the heart to the hands and feet. That is God's grace in action.

Loving God, thank you for the exciting story of the global growth of your church. By your grace may your gospel grow and bear fruit in me and through me. Amen

STEPHEN RAND

A prayer worth praying

For this reason, since the day we heard about you, we have not stopped praying for you. We continually ask God to fill you with the knowledge of his will through all the wisdom and understanding that the Spirit gives, so that you may live a life worthy of the Lord and please him in every way: bearing fruit in every good work, growing in the knowledge of God, being strengthened with all power according to his glorious might so that you may have great endurance and patience, and giving joyful thanks to the Father, who has qualified you to share in the inheritance of his holy people in the kingdom of light.

Many years ago a wonderful and formidable African church leader stood in our living room and asked to pray for our eldest daughter. The prayer that followed was awesome: all-encompassing, visionary, prophetic. She finished, and my wife and I felt there was little more to be said. Thirty years later, I'm sure our daughter is still enfolded by the blessing imparted in that moment.

Paul's prayer here is full of depth, with rich phrases of blessing and encouragement. Reflect on the nouns: knowledge, wisdom, understanding, power, endurance and patience. Explore the verbs, the 'doing' words: fill, bearing fruit, growing, being strengthened. Paul longs for them to be blessed, and for that blessing to overflow to others.

The more he prays for these people he has probably never met, the more he is prompted to joyful thanks to the God who has so evidently been at work in their lives.

A friend once visited an elderly lady who had been a member of our church for many years. Before he left he offered to pray for her. He finished, opened his eyes and saw tears running down her cheeks. But she was not upset. It was simply that no one had prayed for her, personally, ever before. What a tragedy.

Praying for others is a wonderful opportunity and a great privilege.

If you are with someone else, read today's verses out loud – but each time it says 'you' say their name instead. Then they can do the same for you. If you are on your own, insert your own name. This prayer is for you!

STEPHEN RAND

From chains and darkness to freedom and light

The Father… has qualified you to share in the inheritance of his holy people in the kingdom of light. For he has rescued us from the dominion of darkness and brought us into the kingdom of the Son he loves, in whom we have redemption, the forgiveness of sins.

When Jesus met Paul on the Damascus road, he gave him his commission: 'I am sending you… to turn them from darkness to light. I want you to turn them from Satan's power to God. I want their sins to be forgiven. They will be forgiven when they believe in me. They will have their place among God's people' (Acts 26:17–18, NIRV).

As Paul dictates his letter, the joyful thanks he feels for the Colossians reflects his own experience. He has been 'converted', literally 'turned round'. He had been travelling in one direction to do evil; now he is heading the opposite way to do good. Jesus and Paul both use stark imagery to describe the difference between being outside and inside God's family: death and life, darkness and light, slavery and freedom, judgement and forgiveness.

This is what God has done for his people. He has made it possible to share in his inheritance; he has rescued them, set them free. The word translated 'redemption' is the word used to describe the liberation of the people of Israel from Egypt. It also links with the word for 'forgiveness' the payment of a debt, the clearing of the account.

Many of the Jews living in Colossae were descendants of those who had been uprooted from Babylon and moved there by order of the king. They had been transferred, exchanging one kingdom for another. God transfers us to the kingdom of his beloved Son, wipes the slate clean and sets us free. No wonder Paul is full of joyful thanks! The good news is that, to use a football analogy, the transfer window is still open.

The transfer is a cross-border operation: a Christian lives in a new kingdom, under a new authority, with new citizenship – and is made one of the king's family.

STEPHEN RAND

In him, through him, for him

The Son is the image of the invisible God, the firstborn over all creation. For in him all things were created: things in heaven and on earth, visible and invisible, whether thrones or powers or rulers or authorities; all things have been created through him and for him... And he is the head of the body, the church; he is the beginning and the firstborn from among the dead, so that in everything he might have the supremacy.

As a Cambridge history student, I heard a memorable first-week lecture by Walter Ullmann. He emphasised that the key feature of the Middle Ages was that it was Christocentric – it revolved around people's understanding of Christ.

Paul is writing to a church where he knows many are struggling to comprehend exactly who Jesus is and his place in their understanding of God and of life. But he doesn't tell them off, and he doesn't start a theological debate; he quotes a hymn to them.

It's a hymn of beauty and of truth. Above all, it exalts Christ. It is the most complete and absolute endorsement of Jesus as the Son of God. The whole universe is created and sustained by him; all of time revolves around him; the whole created order, all the rulers of this world and all otherworldly spiritual forces are subject to him.

He is also the head of the church. Many Greeks believed that the cosmos was like a body directed by wisdom (*logos*) as the head. Paul believes the universal church is a body receiving purpose and direction from Christ, the living Word (John 1:1). Jesus is not just someone Christians worship on a Sunday. Paul's understanding is that he is at the centre of the whole universe, the meaning of life. Everything is in him, through him and for him. In everything he has the supremacy.

This majestic, all-powerful, cosmic force is a person who knows you, loves you and cares for you. Isn't that just amazing?

STEPHEN RAND

Making peace

For God was pleased to have all his fullness dwell in him, and through him to reconcile to himself all things, whether things on earth or things in heaven, by making peace through his blood, shed on the cross. Once you were alienated from God and were enemies in your minds because of your evil behaviour. But now he has reconciled you by Christ's physical body through death to present you holy in his sight, without blemish and free from accusation – if you continue in your faith, established and firm, and do not move from the hope held out in the gospel.

The first sentence of today's passage forms the last verse of the hymn. It continues the theme of the wholeness and completeness found in Christ and restored through Christ. He is divine – literally the one where all of God is at home. And through his blood shed on the cross all of the universe is reconciled, brought into harmony.

Paul has a clear understanding that the sin of Eve and Adam (Genesis 3) has affected not only the whole human race but the whole of creation. The perfect peace and harmony (*shalom*) of the garden of Eden – where human beings lived in positive and beneficial relationship with God, with the environment (creation), with each other and with themselves – was shattered by sin. But all the brokenness was restored by the death of Jesus. 'The new creation has come' (2 Corinthians 5:17, NIV).

Having finished quoting the hymn, Paul emphasises two things that flow from the understanding of who Jesus is and what he has done (and is doing).

First, each individual in the church is included in the cosmic act of reconciliation. Each rebellious enemy of God has been cleaned up, made perfect, with all charges not only dropped but completely forgotten.

Second, this glorious turnaround will only be realised if they remain rooted and steadfast in their faith. God has done his part; they have to complete theirs.

The cross is the symbol of the Christian faith because it is the place where the whole future of the universe – and the future of all who believe and walk by faith – was changed.

STEPHEN RAND

How to live life

So then, just as you received Christ Jesus as Lord, continue to live your lives in him, rooted and built up in him, strengthened in the faith as you were taught, and overflowing with thankfulness.

Possibly the earliest creed was the simple statement 'Jesus Christ is Lord.' It could also be a very dangerous statement. The Roman authorities were demanding that submission to Rome was bound to a person: the require-ment was to state 'Caesar is Lord.' But Paul's description of becoming a Christian emphasises that it is more than a statement, a form of words; it is entering a personal relationship. A Christian is someone who has 'received' Christ. Their life has been united with his.

Once this profound start has been made, then it has to continue. It's a journey. The Greek word translated 'continue to live' literally means 'walk'. So many people think being a Christian is believing certain things: you qualify if you can tick enough boxes on a theological checklist. It's much more about reaching out to accept Christ's hand offered to you, then walking on hand in hand together in the journey of life.

Were you taught grammar? Few regard it as the most exciting aspect of education, and many have avoided it altogether! But this is one of those verses in the Bible where understanding the grammar fills out the mean-ing of Paul's words. 'Rooted' is in the perfect tense: a present state that is the result of a past action. Paul's analogy is of a plant – it was rooted, and because of that it is still growing. But immediately the analogy changes to a building. 'Built up' is the present tense, implying continuous action. The more a building is built up, the stronger it becomes.

Commentators discuss whether Paul means 'strengthened in faith' or 'strengthened by faith'. I suspect he means both! As we live by faith and exercise faith, so our faith is strengthened and we move on, walking by faith. This is God's doing. That's why we should be 'overflowing with thankfulness'.

Strong Christians aren't those who remind themselves constantly how well they have done; they are the ones who know that without God's presence they would be catastrophic failures.

STEPHEN RAND

Fullness

For in Christ all the fullness of the Deity lives in bodily form, and in Christ you have been brought to fullness.

Paul is now at the heart of his efforts to combat the false teaching that is gaining space in the church at Colossae. First he boldly and straightforwardly states that Jesus was – and is – fully divine. The Living Bible puts it succinctly: 'all of God in a human body'.

I love Christmas. I loathe the Christmas tat in the shops in August. I loathe discovering that half the strings of lights don't work and trying every bulb in the vain hope that this may be the one. But I love Christmas. One reason is that at some point I am reminded that it all started with a baby: the incarnation, God in bodily form. 'Everything of God gets expressed in him, so you can see and hear him clearly,' is how Eugene Peterson puts Colossians 2:9 in *The Message*.

But this reality about Christ creates a reality for you and me as well. The Christian is 'in Christ' and therefore all that fullness of God becomes part of our experience and part of our life. All his love, all his grace, all his mercy, all his power, is available to us. The work of God's Spirit in our lives brings us to fullness – the kind of human beings that God always intended us to be.

I am 'brought to fullness' – many translations say 'made complete'. It is a feature of our contemporary society that most people feel self-sufficient; they have no need of God. But some feel deeply that there is something missing, a gap in the meaning and experience of life. Rock singer Freddie Mercury said, 'You can have everything in the world and still be the loneliest man… Success has brought me world idolisation and millions of pounds. But it's prevented me from having the one thing we all need: a loving, ongoing relationship.' A relationship with Jesus Christ makes us complete.

Lord Jesus Christ, help me to understand more of your fullness, and to see it expressed in my life, day by day, as I walk with you.

STEPHEN RAND

Triumph!

When you were dead in your sins and in the uncircumcision of your flesh, God made you alive with Christ. He forgave us all our sins, having cancelled the charge of our legal indebtedness, which stood against us and condemned us; he has taken it away, nailing it to the cross. And having disarmed the powers and authorities, he made a public spectacle of them, triumphing over them by the cross.

The church at Colossae was clearly made up largely of Gentiles (non-Jews), described here not only as uncircumcised, but spiritually dead and morally bankrupt. Harsh!

The New Testament is brutal but consistent. Whether Jew or Gentile, outside of a relationship with Jesus Christ there is no hope – that person is as good as dead. 'The wages of sin is death' (Romans 6:23, NIV). But God is the resurrection God! He has 'made you alive with Christ'. To make it possible for people to share in the resurrection life of Christ, the barrier had to be destroyed: he forgave all our sins.

Paul elaborates on this using a word unique to this verse, translated here as 'the charge of our legal indebtedness'. It seems the word referred to a handwritten document detailing the precise nature and amount of a debt – an elaborate form of IOU. Paul is emphasising the comprehensive nature of what Jesus did through his death. The handwriting was erased, rubbed out completely, then the document was taken away and nailed to the cross – rendered null and void.

The analogy then switches to a Roman reality. When a victorious general returned to Rome he held a triumph: the defeated enemy was forced to walk into the city in chains, a public spectacle of their defeat and the victor's triumph. On the cross Jesus defeated all the forces of evil comprehensively and completely. The private reality of our sins forgiven, our new life and our liberation was made public, clear for all to see. A triumph!

Do you struggle to believe you can ever be forgiven? Imagine a sheet of paper covered in your own handwriting, detailing all the things that you can't forgive yourself for. Then imagine the nail-pierced hand of Jesus carefully rubbing out every trace, until the page is spotless once again.

STEPHEN RAND

Hearts and minds… on things above

Since, then, you have been raised with Christ, set your hearts on things above, where Christ is, seated at the right hand of God. Set your minds on things above, not on earthly things. For you died, and your life is now hidden with Christ in God. When Christ, who is your life, appears, then you also will appear with him in glory.

Here's the turning point in the letter. Paul has set out his teaching about Jesus and all that Jesus achieved through his death and resurrection; now he turns to what that means for the way those who have received new life in Christ actually live. Paul's emphasis on getting doctrine right is so that doing what is right will follow. It is never an end in itself.

The instruction is to 'set your hearts/minds on things above'. The verb has two different meanings. The first is to seek out, to strive after; the second is to savour or to be like-minded. Both suggest effort, intensity, focus. Together they reinforce this: hearts and minds, the whole being, concentrating 'on things above'.

But what are those things? Does Paul want Christians to wander about in a dreamy, otherworldly daze? Surely not. I think the clue is the contrast with 'earthly things'. These are the things that are temporary, not everlasting. They are also the things which elsewhere in the New Testament are seen as immoral.

Paul is urging his readers that as citizens of heaven they should live out the values of the kingdom in their daily life. They are not being told to be so heavenly minded that they are of no earthly use; rather the instruction is to strive to bring heaven down to earth – living lovingly, graciously, forgivingly, kindly. Live like citizens of heaven, because that is what you are, and what you will be.

The Message puts it like this: 'Don't shuffle along, eyes to the ground, absorbed with the things right in front of you. Look up, and be alert to what is going on around Christ – that's where the action is. See things from *his* perspective.'

The more I focus on Jesus, the more I will behave like Jesus.

STEPHEN RAND

United in Christ

Here there is no Gentile or Jew, circumcised or uncircumcised, barbarian, Scythian, slave or free, but Christ is all, and is in all.

I love this verse. I feel it should be written in large letters on the walls of every church – inside and outside – to remind all those who meet to worship that their unity in Christ is far, far more important than any earthly division, and to tell everyone who passes the building that this is the reality of the church universal, and hopefully every individual church.

Of course, 'here' does not refer to a church building. It means that in the new humanity that God has created, among the citizens of heaven, the dominant feature and common ground is that all have received new life in Christ – that is the basis of their unity.

The first division – between Gentile and Jew – relates to nationality and culture; the second – circumcised or uncircumcised – relates to ethnicity and religion. Scythians were thought of as even more barbarian than the Barbarians – rough and rude, uncultured. Finally, the greatest social divide – between slaves and free citizens – is also bridged. No group is missed out; no one is to be excluded, because 'God so loved the world' (John 3:16, NIV). That's everyone. No exceptions.

As the Living Bible translates it, 'In this new life one's nationality or race or education or social position is unimportant; such things mean nothing. Whether a person has Christ is what matters, and he is equally available to all.' If only the church truly reflected this. Most congregations in the UK are comprised of like-minded people – people like us. This is often because people choose a church on the basis of the worship service – those who like liturgy separate from those who prefer rock-music worship.

But we need to keep working hard to ensure that people of all ethnicities and all social and educational backgrounds are accepted and valued in our churches. I still shudder when I recall someone in the church I attended saying, 'That's not the kind of person we want in our church.'

'Make me a channel of your peace' (from a prayer by St Francis).

STEPHEN RAND

Love as you are loved

Therefore, as God's chosen people, holy and dearly loved, clothe yourselves with compassion, kindness, humility, gentleness and patience. Bear with each other and forgive one another if any of you has a grievance against someone. Forgive as the Lord forgave you. And over all these virtues put on love, which binds them all together in perfect unity.

Did you know that there is a dress code in the kingdom of heaven? It's nothing like the formal night on a cruise ship (thank goodness), Ladies Day at Ascot or even dress-down Friday. Instead, it's surprisingly transparent. That's because it is a set of virtues, a pattern of behaviour. It will be obvious to everyone you meet if you are wearing the right clothes. Compassion, kindness, humility, gentleness and patience are all public virtues – if you are not modelling them, people know.

This clothing is to be put on by 'God's chosen people' – literally, 'the elect'. By using the term here, Paul emphasises that in taking the initiative in building his church, God sets the standard which his people must follow. It is a deep tragedy of history that those who have been most convinced about their 'chosen-ness' have often struggled most to demonstrate their love for those not yet chosen.

These virtues are the very ones we most associate with God himself. He is the essence of compassion, kindness and gentleness – love. Of course, if we are living his new life in us, then we will become like him. Children reflect their carer's behaviour patterns. Many Christians emphasise that the primary task of the Holy Spirit is to make us more like Jesus.

Paul makes this link explicit when he writes, 'Forgive as the Lord forgave you.' Some of us find this the greatest challenge of all – after all, the Lord forgave us graciously, completely, unconditionally. It's relatively easy to love those we don't know well. It is much more difficult to forgive those close to us who have hurt us deeply. But that is what God has done for me and for you.

'Forgive us our sins as we forgive those who sin against us.'

STEPHEN RAND

Wives and husbands

Wives, submit yourselves to your husbands, as is fitting in the Lord. Husbands, love your wives and do not be harsh with them.

'Household rules' are a common feature of Paul's letters. They are part of the outworking of his teaching: if Jesus is Lord, then this has implications for the whole of our lives – the private life as well as the public life. Note that the instruction to wives is to behave 'as is fitting in the Lord'.

It is also clear that in the early church there was a danger that the freedom experienced in Christ could spill over into the rejection of restraints and constraints that were not just conventions of society, but part of the framework of order in which freedom was to be enjoyed. Order in the church is also a common feature of Paul's letters.

The situation was undoubtedly complicated by the clash between the traditionally patriarchal Jewish society and the more liberated attitudes of Greek culture. It is in that context that a careful study of the New Testament will reveal that Jesus and Paul completely undermined patriarchy and established gender equality. In marriage there was to be mutuality, not domination: this is clearest in Ephesians 5:21, where the defining statement in the equivalent section of the letter is 'Submit to one another out of reverence for Christ.'

This mutuality is reinforced by the instruction for husbands to love their wives. In Ephesians again (5:25), they are to love their wives as Christ loved the church: the standard can hardly be set higher. It is tragic that there are still churches where wives (and women in general) are treated unequally. A friend of mine was being physically abused by her husband. When she left him for her own safety, the church allowed him to continue as a member but not her.

Wives and husbands together should work to make the home a safe and loving place. As the old saying goes, 'the rule of love is always better than the love of rule'.

Loving Father, strengthen Christian marriages so that the living out of mutuality and love will witness to your love. Encourage those for whom today's reading has provoked thoughts of pain, sadness or regret.

STEPHEN RAND

Working with all your heart

Whatever you do, work at it with all your heart, as working for the Lord, not for human masters, since you know that you will receive an inheritance from the Lord as a reward. It is the Lord Christ you are serving.

When Paul moves on to instructions for slaves and masters, it is inevitable – and quite right – that we struggle. Paul has been describing how Jesus has brought a new humanity, but he does not seem to have brought a new social order.

First, it is worth noting just how subversive the early church was – slaves were persons, not property, and could enjoy all the same spiritual benefits and status within the church as their masters. But it also seems that the expectation that Jesus would return in their lifetime undermined any drive to change society at that point. And while we celebrate the fact that eventually Christians took up the challenge and fought against slavery, Christians often were their main opponents!

Paul's statement of principle is, nevertheless, applicable to us today. It is a principle that applies to 'whatever you do'. It is not restricted to paid employment. Whether you are the CEO of a large corporation, a worker on the shop floor, a full-time parent or carer, a volunteer – whatever you do, 'work at it with all your heart, as working for the Lord'.

What does this mean in practice? I think it suggests that all our activity should be characterised by integrity, thoughtfulness for others, concern for quality, positivity rather than cynicism and, above all, love. The way we do things should testify to God's love. In *The Practice of the Presence of God*, first published in 1693, Brother Lawrence writes, 'We ought not to be weary of doing little things for the love of God, who regards not the greatness of the work, but the love with which it is performed.'

You may feel undervalued and unappreciated, whether in paid work or voluntary activity. But there is one who knows of all your efforts – the presence of God ensures that nothing goes unnoticed and unappreciated.

---

*Dear God, help me to do all that I do in a way that honours you
and encourages others. Amen*

STEPHEN RAND

21

Always full of grace

Devote yourselves to prayer, being watchful and thankful. And pray for us, too, that God may open a door for our message, so that we may proclaim the mystery of Christ, for which I am in chains. Pray that I may proclaim it clearly, as I should. Be wise in the way you act towards outsiders; make the most of every opportunity. Let your conversation be always full of grace, seasoned with salt, so that you may know how to answer everyone.

As Paul starts to close his letter, he has a few names to mention and detailed instructions to pass on. But first, there is this final, more general set of instructions.

'Devote yourselves to prayer.' How we struggle with this today. Prayer is so easily squeezed out of orders of service, and so easily squeezed out of our everyday lives. Church prayer meetings are increasingly a thing of the past – in the UK at least. My experience is that where people have so much less they look to God so much more. Sometimes it is only in the face of disaster that we remember to pray.

Paul may be in prison because of his preaching, but he still longs for an open door for the message of the love of Christ. He wants everyone to know about it – and he wants the Colossians to care so much about sharing that message that they do it thoughtfully and carefully.

If you are known as a Christian, you are a witness to your faith whether or not you want to be. What we do and what we say will be noticed; it is vital that our actions back our words – and vice versa. But our actions will always speak loudest. Christians, especially leaders, who fail spectacularly get the most publicity.

Our conversation should be 'seasoned with salt' – palatable, flavoursome and bringing out the best of the content. Above all, it should be 'full of grace'. We should share our faith gently, respectfully, in a way that reveals and demonstrates God's love.

Keep reminding me, Lord, that all I am is the result of your love and your grace – then that will be what I share with others.

STEPHEN RAND

Forgiveness in the gospels

Recently, I visited some family members. We had a wonderful time of catching up and enjoying some fun adventures together. But living in close proximity for a fortnight, we experienced a few things for which we needed to forgive each other. I reflected afterwards about this aspect of our visit, for it had been a very good time of relating. And yet, we all are sinful people and thus, even in the good times, we need to forgive the unintentional slights or the words uttered that should have been held back. When we extend forgiveness to each other, the slate becomes clean.

During this fortnight we will explore this core message of Jesus through his teaching and his acts of healing in which he extends forgiveness. His gift reverberates through the four gospels, exemplified through his life, death and resurrection. Indeed, as we will see, at the start of his ministry Jesus proclaims forgiveness, and after he dies and comes back to life, appearing to the disciples in the locked room, he empowers them to extend forgiveness to others. So we will see how this freeing topic is woven into the story of Jesus – and thus into the lives of those who follow him.

We may take for granted how powerful forgiveness can be, until perhaps we find ourselves in need of forgiveness ourselves. But God the Father always extends this gift to his children through the sacrifice of his Son and through the empowering of the Holy Spirit. We no longer have to hold grudges against those who have said nasty things about us or those who have betrayed us. For when we hold on to the sins committed against us, we become bound in a prison of unforgiveness, in which bitterness seems to multiply.

If you'd like to engage with the topic throughout the Old and New Testaments, you could read my BRF Lent book, *The Living Cross: Exploring God's gift of freedom and new life* (2016). It includes questions for discussion and some spiritual exercises to engage with individually or in a small group.

I pray that you will be enriched through this look at Jesus' message of forgiveness.

AMY BOUCHER PYE

The good news of forgiveness

The beginning of the good news about Jesus the Messiah, the Son of God, as it is written in Isaiah the prophet: 'I will send my messenger ahead of you, who will prepare your way' – 'a voice of one calling in the wilderness, "Prepare the way for the Lord, make straight paths for him."' And so John the Baptist appeared in the wilderness, preaching a baptism of repentance for the forgiveness of sins. The whole Judean countryside and all the people of Jerusalem went out to him. Confessing their sins, they were baptised by him in the River Jordan.

As Mark starts his gospel, he cites several Old Testament scriptures that his readers would have known intimately as he declares that Jesus the Messiah is the Lord for whom they have been longing. From the very beginning, Mark emphasises how in Jesus people will find forgiveness of sins through repentance. Thus Mark shows that the Christian story cannot be told without the crucial component of forgiveness. And, importantly, it's a narrative of good news.

Note that John the Baptist, who heralded the coming of Jesus, appears with his message in the wilderness. In the Old Testament, the wilderness could be a place of new beginnings, such as when God drew the Israelites out of Egypt into the promised land. But it was also a place of testing; because of their sins, the Israelites had to wander there for 40 years before they could enter the land God was giving them.

We might feel that we're wandering in our own period of wilderness, and that seeking or extending forgiveness seems excruciating or impossible. But as we ask God through his Spirit to help us, he will give us strength and courage to take the next step. We might not leave our wilderness straight away, but we will know God's guiding hand and his peace and grace.

Forgiving Father, self-sacrificing Son, convicting Holy Spirit, thank you for the gift of forgiveness. Help me to receive and accept the love you impart to me through it, that I may journey into freedom and new life.

AMY BOUCHER PYE

Good news of the kingdom

At that time Jesus came from Nazareth in Galilee and was baptised by John in the Jordan. Just as Jesus was coming up out of the water, he saw heaven being torn open and the Spirit descending on him like a dove. And a voice came from heaven: 'You are my Son, whom I love; with you I am well pleased.'… Jesus went into Galilee, proclaiming the good news of God. 'The time has come,' he said. 'The kingdom of God has come near. Repent and believe the good news!'

Our story moves from John the Baptist to the person he was heralding: Jesus – he who is divine yet condescended to become a man that he could usher in salvation. That he is baptised by John – a mere man – illustrates his humility. That his Father pronounces him as his Son confirms Jesus' divine nature. This combination of being both God and human gives Jesus the power to break the bonds of sin through his death on the cross.

Jesus goes into Galilee, spreading God's good news. The time is now, he says; don't miss the kingdom of God. 'Repent and believe!' His proclamation shapes his time on earth through his message of healing, his call to repentance and his extension of forgiveness. That's good news.

Do we live out this message of repentance in the kingdom of God? Some days we might feel like we have to embrace joy through our will and determination, for our emotions aren't leading the way. For instance, before I sat down to write this I felt slighted when I learned I wasn't invited to a social gathering of some friends. Facing the exclusion, I seemed to have a choice. I could stew and become bitter, imagining a deeper rejection than probably was intended. Or I could look to God for comfort, asking him to heal my hurt feelings and to keep me from sinning while I considered how I could bring joy to those friends.

The good news of Jesus will encompass all of our lives, if we welcome him to be with us.

Father God, you sent your Son that I might experience the fullness of life. Help me to embrace your kingdom throughout all the moments of my day.

AMY BOUCHER PYE

The release of forgiveness

[Jesus] went to Nazareth, where he had been brought up, and on the Sabbath day he went into the synagogue, as was his custom. He stood up to read, and the scroll of the prophet Isaiah was handed to him. Unrolling it, he found the place where it is written: 'The Spirit of the Lord is on me, because he has anointed me to proclaim good news to the poor. He has sent me to proclaim freedom for the prisoners and recovery of sight for the blind, to set the oppressed free, to proclaim the year of the Lord's favour.'... He began by saying to them, 'Today this scripture is fulfilled in your hearing.'

Jesus starts off his public ministry at a synagogue service on the sabbath. He reads from the appointed text, which is from Isaiah (61:1–2), to announce that salvation has come to God's people. 'Today,' he says, 'this scripture is fulfilled in your hearing.'

As the Messiah, Jesus claims the anointing of the Lord, the holy one, in his mission to preach the good news to the poor – the poor in all senses of the word, including the poor in spirit. We see in his message that he implies forgiveness as well, since in the New Testament the same word for proclaiming freedom for the prisoners is used for 'forgive'. Jesus promises to bring sight to the blind and to set the oppressed free.

We might not realise just how radical Jesus was, nor how much he upset the status quo. The religious teachers found it hard to believe that he was the long-awaited Messiah, so they hardened their hearts and rejected his message. Their response, unfortunately, has been repeated throughout history. Some choose to follow him, but some do not.

We who seek to follow Jesus will experience the release of forgiveness. No longer will we be hindered by the prison of bitterness, where our countenance is marred by a permanent scowl and we believe the lies of the enemy.

Thank you, Lord, for setting me free from the chains that keep me bound to the old way of life. Help me to live out your gift of freedom.

AMY BOUCHER PYE

The love of a friend

Some men came, bringing... a paralysed man... Since they could not get him to Jesus because of the crowd, they made an opening in the roof above Jesus by digging through it and then lowered the mat the man was lying on. When Jesus saw their faith, he said to the paralysed man, 'Son, your sins are forgiven.' Now some teachers of the law were sitting there, thinking to themselves, 'Why does this fellow talk like that? He's blaspheming! Who can forgive sins but God alone?'... 'I want you to know that the Son of Man has authority on earth to forgive sins.' So he said to the man, 'I tell you, get up, take your mat and go home.'

The power of love as revealed through our friends can bring healing and forgiveness, as we see in this story. Although we may find the dismantling of the house concerning, with the man's friends lowering him through the roof, we need not worry. Homes at that time and in that place would sport roofs made of timber and reeds, which could be easily repaired.

We might also be surprised to hear that Jesus pronounces the man's sins forgiven as he heals him, a statement that raises the hackles of the religious leaders. Knowing that in the Hebrew scriptures the only source of forgiveness is God, they wonder what Jesus means by this statement. If he can forgive sins, he must not only be deluded, but blasphemous.

Sensing their thoughts, Jesus addresses the controversy head-on through his words and by his actions. When he heals the paralysed man, the man takes up his mat and walks out of the house. He is free, but the teachers remain imprisoned in their unbelief.

This is a tricky passage, especially if we equate healing with forgiveness, believing those who suffer from disease or illness must be hiding some unconfessed sins. If that was true, I reckon we'd all be flat on our back with illness. Suffering, unfortunately, is part of living in the fallen world.

As we have seen, sometimes Jesus heals physical ailments. We can trust, however, that always he will forgive.

Father God, help me to believe that you can bring healing and forgiveness.
I know you are good and that you love me.

AMY BOUCHER PYE

Welcoming sinners

After this, Jesus went out and saw a tax collector by the name of Levi sitting at his tax booth. 'Follow me,' Jesus said to him, and Levi got up, left everything and followed him. Then Levi held a great banquet for Jesus at his house, and a large crowd of tax collectors and others were eating with them. But the Pharisees and the teachers of the law who belonged to their sect complained to his disciples, 'Why do you eat and drink with tax collectors and sinners?' Jesus answered them, 'It is not the healthy who need a doctor, but those who are ill. I have not come to call the righteous, but sinners to repentance.'

Jesus does not restrict his love and acceptance to those at the centre of society, but reaches out to those seen as pariahs, such as tax collectors. Note that in this encounter with Levi, Jesus is the one who takes the initiative. He doesn't shy away from welcoming a person in a hated role to follow him, even though the teachers of the law will object.

And they do. But Jesus reveals the state of their hearts in his reply, for he knows that although they think they are well and thriving, in fact they are sinners in need of repentance. He doesn't let social boundaries keep him from reaching out in love – not only to tax collectors, but, if they would respond, to the teachers of the law also.

We might consciously or subconsciously divide up people into segments of society, thinking that some are welcome at God's feast while others are not. But Jesus explodes these prejudices, showing here and elsewhere how he loves the rich and the poor – and everyone in between.

Perhaps today we can ask God to help us examine our hearts and minds to see if we hold any hidden prejudices against those who are not like us. Once exposed, these thoughts can then be removed from us with God's help.

'You have searched me, Lord, and you know me. You know when I sit and when I rise; you perceive my thoughts from afar… Before a word is on my tongue you, Lord, know it completely' (Psalm 139:1–2, 4, NIV).

AMY BOUCHER PYE

'But I tell you...'

'You have heard that it was said to the people long ago, "You shall not murder, and anyone who murders will be subject to judgement." But I tell you that anyone who is angry with a brother or sister will be subject to judgement. Again, anyone who says to a brother or sister, "Raca," is answerable to the court. And anyone who says, "You fool!" will be in danger of the fire of hell. Therefore, if you are offering your gift at the altar and there remember that your brother or sister has something against you, leave your gift there in front of the altar. First go and be reconciled to them; then come and offer your gift.'

The sermon on the mount covers three chapters in Matthew's gospel, as Jesus speaks to his disciples on a mountain and calls them to carry out his commission to share the good news. He teaches on forgiveness, instructing them how to pray for forgiveness, which we'll look at tomorrow. Before this, he shares the beatitudes, which are words of blessing, and some teaching on how to interpret the wisdom of the law in the Old Testament.

Jesus seeks to correct misinterpretations of the law as he promotes good relations between people. Although someone might not murder, they could disregard another through their anger or insults ('Raca' is a transliteration of an Aramaic term that implies empty-headedness). He names these sins and tells them to seek reconciliation before offering any gifts at the altar.

Little slights and outright name-calling can be something we experience from our friends, family and neighbours. Or indeed, we might find ourselves being the ones slinging the mud. As we turn to God, we can ask him to release us from the power of stinging words. We might think that they are only words, but their power can shape us for good or for ill. May the Lord give us forgiveness and hope as we dwell in peace and unity with those whom we meet.

Lord God, please help me to guard my mouth today, that nothing displeasing to you comes out of it. Help me build up someone today with words that edify.

AMY BOUCHER PYE

Forgive as you've been forgiven

'This, then, is how you should pray: "Our Father in heaven, hallowed be your name, your kingdom come, your will be done, on earth as it is in heaven. Give us today our daily bread. And forgive us our debts, as we also have forgiven our debtors. And lead us not into temptation, but deliver us from the evil one." For if you forgive other people when they sin against you, your heavenly Father will also forgive you. But if you do not forgive others their sins, your Father will not forgive your sins.'

Regularly we may pray this most famous prayer of Jesus. But as we do so, we may not consider that we are asking the Lord to forgive those who wrong us, just as he forgives us. Do we think through the implications – that if we do not forgive that person, we ourselves might not be forgiven? I've probably prayed the Lord's prayer many times without considering the deeper consequences. (It's important to note, however, that many biblical commentators agree that our salvation isn't on the line if we don't forgive. However, if we don't, we end up being affected by an unforgiving attitude.)

As I consider this prayer, I think about someone in my life who keeps on spreading hurt and lies. I've taken measures to limit this wrongdoing, but because of the circumstances I'm not able to be completely free. What I find most challenging in this situation is the question of whether I can keep on forgiving their bad behaviour. Can I extend the grace that God extends to me? Can I lose the need to pay them back for their sins?

Some days I stew in bitterness, but when I heed the call of God's gentle Holy Spirit, I bring to him my anger, pain and feelings of hurt. I then can be released from these difficult feelings, knowing that God is the ultimate judge and that I don't need to put myself in his place.

If you need to extend forgiveness today, I pray you will be given strength, courage and grace, that you might be able to pray the Lord's prayer with joy and freedom.

Lord Jesus Christ, son of the living God, have mercy on me, a sinner.

AMY BOUCHER PYE

Lavish love

'Do you see this woman? I came into your house. You did not give me any water for my feet, but she wet my feet with her tears and wiped them with her hair. You did not give me a kiss, but this woman, from the time I entered, has not stopped kissing my feet. You did not put oil on my head, but she has poured perfume on my feet. Therefore, I tell you, her many sins have been forgiven – as her great love has shown. But whoever has been forgiven little loves little.' Then Jesus said to her, 'Your sins are forgiven.'

Jesus continues exploding the erroneous beliefs of those whom he meets. Although the Pharisee Simon welcomed him to dine in his home, he didn't extend the normal courtesies of anointing Jesus' head with oil or washing his feet. But a woman who entered the door, which was open as per the custom with meals held for important guests, showered Jesus with love. Jesus makes the point that this so-called sinful woman loves deeply because she has been freed from her many sins.

As a Pharisee, Simon would have been shocked to hear Jesus proclaim her forgiven of her sins. For, as I alluded to previously, in Jewish thought only God can forgive sins. The fact that Jesus forgives her sins means he equates himself with God. And he heralds the coming of a new era of grace in which not only does he forgive others, but ordinary people can extend forgiveness to their wrongdoers too. In the Hebrew scriptures, this simply was not done.

When we fail spectacularly, we might easily relate to the forgiven woman. When we think we're doing OK, however, we might forget the gift of forgiveness and think we're entitled to the blessings God gives us. Why not take a few minutes to ponder where you might fall on the spectrum – do you find yourself closer to the woman or to Simon?

May God's forgiveness wash us clean and anoint us with joy and hope.

'In him we have redemption through his blood, the forgiveness of sins, in accordance with the riches of God's grace that he lavished on us'
(Ephesians 1:7–8, NIV).

AMY BOUCHER PYE

Unending forgiveness

Then Peter came to Jesus and asked, 'Lord, how many times shall I forgive my brother or sister who sins against me? Up to seven times?' Jesus answered, 'I tell you, not seven times, but seventy-seven times.

She had left her husband for another man. I gasped in surprise as I read the contribution to my weekly website series called 'Forgiveness Fridays'. I know the writer professionally and personally, and would not have guessed that some two decades previously she had tried to set up a new life with a man not her husband. After two weeks, he decided to return to his wife, and left the woman bereft. Without much thought, she called her husband. He agreed to pick her up and work things out in their marriage.

The contributor speaks of how it took many months and a lot of trust which needed to be rebuilt on both sides of their relationship. They had to forgive not only seven times but seventy-seven times. Their patterns of life had developed into ones in which they both hurt each other regularly, and they had to learn not only to forgive but to develop new ways of living. Forgiveness for them needed to become an integral aspect of their daily lives.

Peter's question to Jesus may seem calculated, but in asking him if seven times of forgiveness is sufficient, Peter is actually going beyond what is required in the Old Testament. For instance, such books as Amos and Job teach that to forgive three times is enough to show mercy. But Jesus expands the answer of how many times we should forgive to that of a number which seems limitless. Because God has forgiven us, we too should forgive those who wrong us.

It seems that in families and other close relationships, we have more than ample opportunity to forgive those close to us. Wronging others seems to come naturally to us, and so we need to employ God's supernatural help to extend to them his grace and mercy. Even seventy-seven times.

Father God, saving Son, loving Spirit, work in and through me,
that I might reflect your love in my daily actions and thoughts.
Help me to bring you glory.

AMY BOUCHER PYE

No longer blind

As [Jesus] went along, he saw a man blind from birth. His disciples asked him, 'Rabbi, who sinned, this man or his parents, that he was born blind?' 'Neither this man nor his parents sinned,' said Jesus, 'but this happened so that the works of God might be displayed in him. As long as it is day, we must do the works of him who sent me. Night is coming, when no one can work. While I am in the world, I am the light of the world.'... So the man went and washed, and came home seeing.

Blindness was a common affliction in Bible times, not least because of the lack of clean water to halt infections. Jesus often healed blind people, making the connection not only to the physical state of blindness but to the spiritual one too. He, the light of the world, came to end all kinds of darkness.

In John's gospel, Jesus heals a man who had been born blind, which to the disciples implies that either he or his parents had done wrong. Jesus corrects them quickly, however, saying that through this ailment God's work would be revealed. Jesus sends the man to cleanse himself, and when he obeys, he is healed.

If you have time to read the whole story in John's gospel, you'll see the controversy that ensues. The teachers of the law press the healed man to find out who healed him. They cannot believe that he could be without sin, or that Jesus is from God. The story illustrates how Jesus can relieve people from their blindness, if they would submit to him and obey. Those like the teachers of the law who reject his teaching remain shrouded in darkness.

I find it hardest to spot my own sins, especially when it comes to matters of pride. The plank in my eye surely obstructs my view of any specks in the eyes of others. But God through Jesus and the Holy Spirit can and will reveal those sins to me – sometimes through a friend or family member. I need not remain in the dark.

'Whether he is a sinner or not, I don't know. One thing I do know.
I was blind but now I see!' (John 9:25, NIV).

AMY BOUCHER PYE

Finding what's lost

Jesus told [the Pharisees and teachers of the law] this parable: 'Suppose one of you has a hundred sheep and loses one of them. Doesn't he leave the ninety-nine in the open country and go after the lost sheep until he finds it? And when he finds it, he joyfully puts it on his shoulders and goes home. Then he calls his friends and neighbours together and says, "Rejoice with me; I have found my lost sheep." I tell you that in the same way there will be more rejoicing in heaven over one sinner who repents than over ninety-nine righteous people who do not need to repent.'

Have you ever searched for something that you've misplaced, becoming almost obsessed by trying to find it? I can think of times of increasing stress and anxiety when I've lost something, depending on the item, and of the amazing joy when what was lost is found. For me and my husband, the longest 20 minutes we have endured was on a German campsite when our three-year-old son wandered off. He couldn't understand why I burst into tears of relief when we found him.

Jesus, in answering the Pharisees and teachers of the law, tells three parables that show the length God goes to in seeking those who are lost. They may have fallen away from him through wrongdoing, but as the parable of the lost son recounts, which follows the gospel passage we're reading today, God continues to search for them. He is the good shepherd who leaves his other 99 sheep to find the one who went astray.

These parables reveal that we don't have to reach a certain state of goodness before God will accept us. Instead, we see how he yearns always for his people to return to him. And when they do, he hosts a fabulous party, for he wants everyone to celebrate.

Today, why not spend some time thinking about, and praying for, anyone whom you'd like to see found by God. We can turn our anxious thoughts into prayer.

Lord God, you've been called the hound of heaven, for you seek and search for those who are lost. Thank you that you'll always find me.

AMY BOUCHER PYE

Unmediated access

When evening came, Jesus and his disciples went out of the city. In the morning, as they went along, they saw the fig-tree withered from the roots. Peter remembered and said to Jesus, 'Rabbi, look! The fig-tree you cursed has withered!' 'Have faith in God,' Jesus answered... 'Therefore I tell you, whatever you ask for in prayer, believe that you have received it, and it will be yours. And when you stand praying, if you hold anything against anyone, forgive them, so that your Father in heaven may forgive you your sins.'

We may wonder why Jesus would curse a fig-tree for not bearing fruit when it was out of season. Looking at this passage in its context will point us to some clues. According to biblical commentators, one suggestion is that Jesus uses the fig-tree to represent the temple where God's people worship. Here the Jewish people offer their prayers, for the Lord promised to dwell in the temple. But Jesus knows that with his death and resurrection, people won't need to limit their prayers to when they are in the temple. Instead, Jesus' death will create a new house of prayer – open to the Jewish people and the Gentiles.

After Jesus' resurrection, faith in God will be sufficient to meet with him. Thus Jesus tells his disciples to pray and to believe – they won't need to offer sacrifices in order to be heard. Also, they should offer forgiveness freely, that God the Father will forgive them.

We may take it for granted that we can pray to God through Jesus and the Holy Spirit without mediation or needing to offer sacrifices. Enjoying the gift of free communication with God is not something I want to deny, but it's good too to step back and ponder the majesty and wonder of God the creator of the universe. He who is unfathomable has made himself approachable to us.

'But will God really dwell on earth? The heavens, even the highest heaven, cannot contain you... Yet give attention to your servant's prayer and his plea for mercy, Lord my God... Hear from heaven, your dwelling place, and when you hear, forgive' (1 Kings 8:27–28, 30, NIV).

AMY BOUCHER PYE

The death of a righteous man

It was now about noon, and darkness came over the whole land until three in the afternoon, for the sun stopped shining. And the curtain of the temple was torn in two. Jesus called out with a loud voice, 'Father, into your hands I commit my spirit.' When he had said this, he breathed his last. The centurion, seeing what had happened, praised God and said, 'Surely this was a righteous man.' When all the people who had gathered to witness this sight saw what took place, they beat their breasts and went away. But all those who knew him, including the women who had followed him from Galilee, stood at a distance, watching these things.

I could not fail to include the story of Jesus' death in a look at forgiveness in the gospels. After all, the death and resurrection of the Son of God ushers in our own forgiveness. Because he is the perfect sacrifice, Jesus satisfies the demands of God's law. Indeed, God in his graciousness offers to us the solution to our problems. In Jesus we find new life.

Good Friday may now seem like a distant memory, so it could be a good time to ponder Jesus' death away from the rigours of Lent. Why not try some imaginative prayer in the style of Ignatius of Loyola (1491–1556) with the passage printed above? Ask God through his Holy Spirit to ignite your imagination as you place yourself at the scene of the cross. Try to picture the landscape and surroundings; take in the crowds and see the darkened sky. As you read through the story, see which character you might become in it, whether one of the disciples or perhaps a soldier. Ask God to reveal something of the narrative through this imaginative process. You might find it helpful to write out your feelings and insights.

Jesus' death on the cross imparts to us forgiveness when we accept the gift of salvation. May we know joy, freedom and wonder at this amazing gift.

Lord Jesus Christ, you who are the Son of God yet came to live as a man on earth: you died that I might live. Help me to understand the magnitude of your sacrifice.

AMY BOUCHER PYE

New life

On the evening of that first day of the week, when the disciples were together, with the doors locked for fear of the Jewish leaders, Jesus came and stood among them and said, 'Peace be with you!' After he said this, he showed them his hands and side. The disciples were overjoyed when they saw the Lord. Again Jesus said, 'Peace be with you! As the Father has sent me, I am sending you.' And with that he breathed on them and said, 'Receive the Holy Spirit. If you forgive anyone's sins, their sins are forgiven; if you do not forgive them, they are not forgiven.'

Their hero died. No doubt the disciples are devastated, and probably bewildered too. What about the kingdom of God that Jesus had been inaugurating? His friends huddle together, locked away and fearing persecution.

But Jesus doesn't want them to stay in hiding. He appears in person to them, confirming that it is him by showing them his scars. After offering them peace and commissioning them in the name of the Father, he breathes the Holy Spirit on them. This gift of the Spirit dwelling within them will help them overcome their fears.

Then Jesus tells them to forgive sins. I find it interesting that his command to forgive is one of the first things he says to the disciples after his resurrection. After all, he knows the power of sin to bind people into prisons of bitterness and disappointment. He wants them – and us – to spread his good news of freedom from sin through the forgiveness of sins.

I pray that this fortnight of reflection on forgiveness in the gospels will spur you on to love and good deeds, and that aspects of Jesus' expression of forgiveness will stick in your mind and heart. May you live free and unhindered in God's guiding love, spreading the pleasing aroma of Christ wherever you go.

Father God, thank you for the gift of new life. Thank you that no longer do I have to be bound in old ways of living. Help me to embrace the gift of forgiveness in all aspects of my daily life, as I bring you glory.

AMY BOUCHER PYE

Water in John

Throughout my Christian life I have found John's gospel incredibly helpful in drawing me closer to Jesus. John's poetic style and evocative use of imagery is easy to relate to, revealing something of both the mystery and the 'earthiness' of Jesus. This series of reflections focuses on the way John uses water to represent the Holy Spirit, promised by Jesus to bring new life, cleansing and renewal. In our first passage, John the Baptist introduces us to Jesus as the Messiah, saviour of the world – and the implications of this unfold through the subsequent passages. We will see Jesus using water for healing and to demonstrate his miraculous powers. But we will also discover more about Jesus as a human being: asking an unlikely woman for a drink to quench his thirst; enjoying a wedding party with family and friends; and washing the feet of his disciples – a human act of service and a prophetic sign pointing towards his death on the cross. In our final reflection, John depicts water as a sign of hope in the context of that tragic death.

We will meet a number of characters, including a woman of dubious background, a Jewish leader and a blind man. They are all very different from each other, and Jesus meets each one according to their individual need. He demonstrates his ability to empathise with what it means to be human, but also to transcend the human condition using miraculous signs and wonders which point to his divinity.

Throughout these passages we will encounter a Jesus who offers himself as the source of living water that can quench every thirst, heal and restore lives. These encounters should challenge us to reflect on our own journey of faith with Jesus – on how we respond to his call on our lives. They are a call to draw nearer to him, to open ourselves up to him, to go deeper with him. And we should be challenged to reflect on how we are being called to share what we receive with those around us. Jesus invites each of us to be open to all that he wants to give us through his Spirit, for our life of service as his followers, so that others can come to know his transforming love.

DEBBIE ORRISS

Water as a sign

The next day he saw Jesus coming towards him and declared, 'Here is the Lamb of God who takes away the sin of the world! This is he of whom I said, "After me comes a man who ranks ahead of me because he was before me." I myself did not know him; but I came baptising with water for this reason, that he might be revealed to Israel.' And John testified, 'I saw the Spirit descending from heaven like a dove, and it remained on him. I myself did not know him, but the one who sent me to baptise with water said to me, "He on whom you see the Spirit descend and remain is the one who baptises with the Holy Spirit." And I myself have seen and have testified that this is the Son of God.'

When I was living in Sheffield I went for a walk as usual across some moorland in the Peak District. I thought I knew the route, but after a while I began to doubt. I was on a footpath – but was it the right one? Then I looked into the distance and could see that the path split into two. Even more confusing! What a relief when I saw a signpost where the footpath divided, showing me the way I needed to go.

In our passage today, we meet John the Baptist, Jesus' cousin, introduced earlier in the chapter as a witness who 'testifies' to Jesus. John's mission is to point to Jesus, and his act of baptism, rather than focusing on water as a symbol of being 'cleansed' from sin, is a sign pointing to Jesus as the Messiah, the Saviour of the world.

Think of people who have been signposts to Jesus for you. How did they 'testify' or point to him? My sense is that perhaps you have experienced something of Jesus' character shining through them by his Spirit – his loving-kindness maybe, or his generosity or unconditional love. Who might God be asking you to be a signpost for, to point them to Jesus?

Lord, help me to be a signpost to Jesus in my life. May my words and actions point away from myself and witness to him, in the power of the Holy Spirit.

DEBBIE ORRISS

Water transformed (part 1)

On the third day there was a wedding in Cana of Galilee, and the mother of Jesus was there. Jesus and his disciples had also been invited to the wedding. When the wine gave out, the mother of Jesus said to him, 'They have no wine.' And Jesus said to her, 'Woman, what concern is that to you and to me? My hour has not yet come.' His mother said to the servants, 'Do whatever he tells you.' Now standing there were six stone water-jars for the Jewish rites of purification, each holding twenty or thirty gallons. Jesus said to them, 'Fill the jars with water.' And they filled them up to the brim. He said to them, 'Now draw some out, and take it to the chief steward.' So they took it.

The wedding at Cana is one of my favourite events in the accounts of Jesus' life and ministry. It illustrates both his divinity and his humanness. Jesus responds to the situation of the wine running out in a miraculous way, demonstrating his power as the Son of God over earthly elements. We'll focus on the miracle of what happens to the water tomorrow; today let's focus on his humanness.

We see Jesus at a wedding, celebrating with his family and friends, being involved in people's everyday lives, having fun! This demonstrates an important and positive aspect of what it is to be human. Sadly, some people outside the Christian faith often have an impression of Christians as killjoys or spoilsports, who focus on what you're 'not supposed to do as a Christian', rather than as people who have discovered and long to share the wonderful, life-giving fullness of the presence of Jesus in their lives. This contradicts our passage today: Jesus, instead of deciding that the guests had drunk enough wine already, was happy to provide more!

How do people in your community perceive your church? As a place of welcome and celebration? Are there opportunities for your church to be involved in local community events of celebration?

Jesus, you entered into the life events of your family and friends and had fun. Help me to experience and demonstrate the 'life in all its fullness' that you offer to all.

DEBBIE ORRISS

Water transformed (part 2)

When the steward tasted the water that had become wine, and did not know where it came from (though the servants who had drawn the water knew), the steward called the bridegroom and said to him, 'Everyone serves the good wine first, and then the inferior wine after the guests have become drunk. But you have kept the good wine until now.' Jesus did this, the first of his signs, in Cana of Galilee, and revealed his glory; and his disciples believed in him.

When I was a youth worker, at the end of the school year I organised a celebration for the volunteers that worked with me in the local schools. I thought I'd arranged for invitations to be sent out in two different colours, one that meant 'bring a savoury course' and the other 'bring a sweet'. I'm not sure what happened to the printing, but everyone brought a pudding! I was very embarrassed. Thankfully, people saw the funny side, and we sent out for fish and chips.

Hospitality was, and still is, a major feature of Middle Eastern culture. So the bridegroom's embarrassment at the wine running out at his wedding party was much worse than mine. Jesus comes to the rescue, and when the water from the stone jars is poured, it has become 'good wine'. This transformation of water into wine is significant: remember that the jars contained water normally used for Jewish purification rites. It speaks of Jesus' death on the cross superseding the law – becoming clean from sin was to happen in a different way from slavishly trying to keep every minute detail of the Jewish law.

Today, many people do believe that trying hard to 'keep the rules' is the way to God. Several TV dramas depict this, with central characters either trying to bargain for God's forgiveness or atone for their sins themselves. Even Christians can slip back into trying to earn forgiveness, rather than trusting in their state of 'forgiven-ness' through Jesus' death on the cross.

Lord, remind me that you have done all that is necessary to restore my relationship with God. Help me to live my life in gratitude and freedom as a result of that wonderful truth.

DEBBIE ORRISS

Water and Spirit

Now there was a Pharisee named Nicodemus, a leader of the Jews. He came to Jesus by night and said to him, 'Rabbi, we know that you are a teacher who has come from God; for no one can do these signs that you do apart from the presence of God.' Jesus answered him, 'Very truly, I tell you, no one can see the kingdom of God without being born from above.' Nicodemus said to him, 'How can anyone be born after having grown old? Can one enter a second time into the mother's womb and be born?' Jesus answered, 'Very truly, I tell you, no one can enter the kingdom of God without being born of water and Spirit.'

In our passage today, we witness a traditional form of conversation between Jewish rabbis (teachers), who would ask questions of each other as a way of developing their ideas about God. Jesus tells Nicodemus that water baptism for repentance of sins isn't enough to enter the kingdom of God. This outward ritual needs to be accompanied by an internal change, a spiritual rebirth.

A couple of years ago I was walking around a reservoir near Sheffield. It rained for most of the way, and I noticed that I was experiencing the rain in different ways. In the open areas of the walk it was raining quite heavily on to me, while under the trees it dripped gently. On some parts of the walk, the water flowed across my path, and on others I could hear it but couldn't see it, because it ran underground.

This walk reminded me of the mystery of the Spirit – we can experience him in many different ways: sometimes very directly, for example when we're singing a particular hymn, and sometimes gently, perhaps while walking by a lake or in the mountains. Maybe we suddenly feel a sense of peace while we're praying. Some of us may have had an initial powerful experience of the Holy Spirit, but no experience is any better than another. Spiritual rebirth needs to happen daily, as we come before Jesus to ask for all that we need for each day.

Lord, help me to be open to the constant,
daily renewing of your Spirit within me.

DEBBIE ORRISS

Water breaks down barriers

[Jesus] came to a Samaritan city called Sychar, near the plot of ground that Jacob had given to his son Joseph. Jacob's well was there, and Jesus, tired out by his journey, was sitting by the well. It was about noon. A Samaritan woman came to draw water, and Jesus said to her, 'Give me a drink.' (His disciples had gone to the city to buy food.) The Samaritan woman said to him, 'How is it that you, a Jew, ask a drink of me, a woman of Samaria?' (Jews do not share things in common with Samaritans.) Jesus answered her, 'If you knew the gift of God, and who it is that is saying to you, 'Give me a drink,' you would have asked him, and he would have given you living water.'

During a previous ministerial role, I served in a church that held weekly lunchtime concerts followed by refreshments. One day at an organ recital, a rather confused woman came in, walked to the organ and tried to sit on the organ seat next to the organist. The organist and I encouraged her to sit on a chair, and the recital continued. She was welcomed by those serving refreshments afterwards and enjoyed a cup of tea before she left. I was moved by the respectful way that people in the church had treated her.

In our passage today, Jesus has gone out of his way to go through Samaria; this is no chance encounter. He uses his thirst for water to begin a conversation with a Samaritan, someone most Jews avoided. Jesus completely ignores the established social and religious attitudes to minister to this woman at her point of need, showing her respect and love. The lady at the organ recital received the same respect and love from those serving refreshments, but through a cup of tea rather than water!

I wonder how many people outside the church feel that there are insurmountable barriers between them and God? What barriers do we consciously or unconsciously put between certain people and the Christian faith?

Lord, help me to accept all people as you do.
Give me the grace I need for those I find difficult.

DEBBIE ORRISS

Water that transforms

The woman said to [Jesus], 'Sir, you have no bucket, and the well is deep. Where do you get that living water? Are you greater than our ancestor Jacob, who gave us the well, and with his sons and his flocks drank from it?' Jesus said to her, 'Everyone who drinks of this water will be thirsty again, but those who drink of the water that I will give them will never be thirsty. The water that I will give will become in them a spring of water gushing up to eternal life.' The woman said to him, 'Sir, give me this water, so that I may never be thirsty or have to keep coming here to draw water.'

A few years ago I did a truck safari into the Turkana desert in Kenya. The group I travelled with brought along lots of bottled water, but the road was bumpy and much of it ended up on the floor of the truck. We were dismayed – we didn't know when our supplies would be replenished. I'm fortunate that this is the only time I have faced potentially serious deprivation of water. Here in the UK fresh water is something I take for granted, but in many parts of the world, including the Middle East, water is a precious commodity because of its scarcity at times.

Jesus offers 'living water' that will always quench our thirst. It is fresh and abundant, gushing up. The power of this image is to some extent lost on those of us who can simply turn on a tap whenever we want. What is this living water? It is everything that Jesus can provide for us at our point of need. This can be spiritual refreshment, help in difficult circumstances or joy in times of trial. It is also the steady sustaining presence of Jesus, throughout our daily lives. Its source is the Holy Spirit, and it is eternal and abundant. We can receive from Jesus as we make time to be with him, listening and simply resting in his presence in an intentional way. We can receive through reading his word and through times of worship, alone and with others.

Lord, in the busyness of life, help me to make time to be with you and receive from you.

DEBBIE ORRISS

Healing waters?

After this there was a festival of the Jews, and Jesus went up to Jerusalem. Now in Jerusalem by the Sheep Gate there is a pool, called in Hebrew Beth-zatha, which has five porticoes. In these lay many invalids – blind, lame, and paralysed. One man was there who had been ill for thirty-eight years. When Jesus saw him lying there and knew that he had been there a long time, he said to him, 'Do you want to be made well?' The sick man answered him, 'Sir, I have no one to put me into the pool when the water is stirred up; and while I am making my way, someone else steps down ahead of me.' Jesus said to him, 'Stand up, take your mat and walk.' At once the man was made well, and he took up his mat and began to walk.

Miraculous healing can be a difficult issue in Christian circles. Some people seem to experience it on a regular basis; others pray faithfully for years with no apparent results; still others experience a significant one-off event that turns their life around for ever. In our passage today, we're told there are many people at this pool needing healing. Why does Jesus go to this man in particular? What is special about the waters at the pool? Do they have healing properties? Amid all these questions, what we do know is that the man is healed, by Jesus not the 'healing waters'. Notice that Jesus treats the man as an individual and asks him if he wants to be made well. Maybe the man had become used to lying by the pool, and perhaps preferred that way of life to the more demanding one that would result from being healed.

How do you react to this event? With joy for the man, or slight feelings of resentment – 'Nothing like that ever happens to me'? Jesus responds to individual need, and we can trust that he knows the needs of each person who comes to him and will respond according to that need.

Lord, thank you that you hear and answer my prayers, for myself and others. Give me the faith to believe this, when it seems that prayers are going unanswered.

DEBBIE ORRISS

Walking on water

When evening came, [Jesus'] disciples went down to the sea, got into a boat, and started across the sea to Capernaum. It was now dark, and Jesus had not yet come to them. The sea became rough because a strong wind was blowing. When they had rowed about three or four miles, they saw Jesus walking on the sea and coming near the boat, and they were terrified. But he said to them, 'It is I; do not be afraid.' Then they wanted to take him into the boat, and immediately the boat reached the land towards which they were going.

I love being by the sea, particularly when it's rough and the waves are crashing into the shore. It speaks powerfully to me of the mighty creativity of God. Earlier in this chapter the people were seeking to take Jesus by force and make him king. Jesus doesn't need human beings to make him king. In this passage, Jesus demonstrates his kingship and power as Son of God by walking on water. Maybe this is why, when he walks towards them on the sea, the disciples are 'terrified' rather than reassured. Perhaps they realise for the first time that Jesus cannot be tamed or contained.

It reminds me of a passage from *The Lion, the Witch and the Wardrobe* by C.S. Lewis: "'Aslan is a lion – the Lion, the great Lion." "Ooh," said Susan. "I'd thought he was a man. Is he – quite safe? I shall feel rather nervous about meeting a lion…" "Safe?" said Mr Beaver… "Who said anything about safe? Course he isn't safe. But he's good. He's the King, I tell you."'

Which Jesus do you most often relate to: the all-powerful king ruling the waves or the ever-present friend who reassures, comforts and guides? Perhaps he is challenging you to encounter him in a way beyond that with which you feel comfortable. It is often when we are pushed beyond our own limits that we encounter Jesus more powerfully and our faith grows stronger.

Lord, forgive me when I become complacent, preferring what is comfortable and safe. Give me faith to take risks in my walk with you, trusting in your power and love.

DEBBIE ORRISS

Thirst quenched

So they said to him, 'What sign are you going to give us then, so that we may see it and believe you? What work are you performing? Our ancestors ate the manna in the wilderness; as it is written, "He gave them bread from heaven to eat."' Then Jesus said to them, 'Very truly, I tell you, it was not Moses who gave you the bread from heaven, but it is my Father who gives you the true bread from heaven. For the bread of God is that which comes down from heaven and gives life to the world.' They said to him, 'Sir, give us this bread always.' Jesus said to them, 'I am the bread of life. Whoever comes to me will never be hungry, and whoever believes in me will never be thirsty.'

Wherever I am in the world, it seems that there is constant pressure to want more and to buy more. Most of the world's economies rely on this state of dissatisfaction, with economic health measured by how much people are spending. I've just had a call from my mobile phone provider, asking me if I want to upgrade my phone, just because there's a newer model available. And I feel really uncomfortable when, having bought something online from a website, similar products then appear on my social media pages, encouraging me to spend more.

Has nothing changed in 2,000 years? Earlier in chapter 6, Jesus fed a large crowd of people with five loaves and two fish, and some of that same crowd are now asking Jesus for a sign to help them believe! They appear not to be satisfied with the miracle they have experienced. What more do they need?

And yet Jesus promises that his followers' spiritual hunger and thirst *will* be satisfied – provided they come to him and believe in him. Perhaps when we do feel spiritually 'dry' it's because we've skimped on our intentional time with Jesus, and our belief has wavered because we've taken our eyes off him and been distracted by other things.

Lord, on those days when I feel 'dry' in my walk with you, help me, through your Holy Spirit, to draw closer to you and renew my faith.

DEBBIE ORRISS

Water ever flowing

On the last day of the festival, the great day, while Jesus was standing there, he cried out, 'Let anyone who is thirsty come to me, and let the one who believes in me drink. As the scripture has said, "Out of the believer's heart shall flow rivers of living water."' Now he said this about the Spirit, which believers in him were to receive; for as yet there was no Spirit, because Jesus was not yet glorified.

Are you easily embarrassed? I find it difficult if someone is drawing attention to themselves in a public space – something to do with my British reserve perhaps! Here Jesus is definitely getting the attention of the crowd as he cries out to them. It is the Festival of Tabernacles, and as part of the ritual water and wine would be poured around the altar and prayers would be said for rain and for the resurrection of the dead. Jesus is using the imagery and ritual of the festival to make some bold claims about himself as the source of living water. He invites believers to come to him to have their thirst quenched, and that invitation extends to us too.

Yet the flow of the Spirit needs to be not just one way. It isn't enough for us to receive this life-giving water from Jesus; as we receive and drink, it should be flowing out from us to others. It is tempting to enjoy times of infilling with Jesus, perhaps in our personal reflection or in uplifting church services, without these times having any effect on the individuals and communities around us. How do you share with others what you have received from Jesus? Perhaps there is a person or community project that the Lord is calling you to share something of his living water with – maybe a message of hope or an act of loving concern. Today could be the day to make a call or a visit that opens the door to sharing Christ in a new way. Trust that through this Jesus will fill you afresh with his life-giving Spirit.

Lord, help me to receive from you this day, and show me
those you want me to bless with the blessings you give me.

DEBBIE ORRISS

Human spit?

As [Jesus] walked along, he saw a man blind from birth. His disciples asked him, 'Rabbi, who sinned, this man or his parents, that he was born blind?' Jesus answered, 'Neither this man nor his parents sinned; he was born blind so that God's works might be revealed in him. We must work the works of him who sent me while it is day; night is coming when no one can work. As long as I am in the world, I am the light of the world.' When he had said this, he spat on the ground and made mud with the saliva and spread the mud on the man's eyes, saying to him, 'Go, wash in the pool of Siloam' (which means Sent). Then he went and washed and came back able to see.

Today's passage uses physical blindness and healing to illustrate the revelation of Jesus as the Son of God. Both his humanity and divinity are powerful aspects of the healing. Jesus uses his ordinary human spit to make the clay that he places on the man's eyes. Then his extraordinary divine power completes the healing.

How does Jesus reveal himself today? I believe people can experience him and his power in ways that can include natural human actions as well as miraculous events. Some time ago, I was involved with a Christian project that worked to support homeless men and women. I witnessed the way that spontaneous acts of loving-kindness by project volunteers transformed the lives of those in need. When I invited one homeless man into church to get warm one cold morning, I witnessed him being physically moved by an experience of the Holy Spirit as he walked into that sacred space. He was quite fearful of what he was feeling, and I gently explained that he was sensing something of God in a place where prayers had been said for centuries.

Sometimes we can go through the day blind to the presence of Jesus, perhaps because we are only looking for the miracles, or maybe because we need the wisdom of someone else to point out Jesus to us.

Lord, please give me eyes to see you at work in my daily life,
and enable me to reveal you in the lives of others.

DEBBIE ORRISS

Water for service

And during supper Jesus, knowing that the Father had given all things into his hands, and that he had come from God and was going to God, got up from the table, took off his outer robe, and tied a towel around himself. Then he poured water into a basin and began to wash the disciples' feet and to wipe them with the towel that was tied around him. He came to Simon Peter, who said to him, 'Lord, are you going to wash my feet?' Jesus answered, 'You do not know now what I am doing, but later you will understand.' Peter said to him, 'You will never wash my feet.' Jesus answered, 'Unless I wash you, you have no share with me.' Simon Peter said to him, 'Lord, not my feet only but also my hands and my head!'

There's nothing special or miraculous about the water used in today's passage. It's just poured into a bowl and used to wash feet covered in the day's mud and dust. But the event wrong-foots (excuse the pun) the disciples, as it happens after their shared meal, whereas foot-washing would normally happen as people entered a house. And what is even more significant is that it's Jesus doing the washing not a household servant: Jesus, the Son of God, who has healed the blind, walked on water and miraculously fed thousands of people.

Peter, in typical fashion, questions what Jesus, his Lord, is doing washing his feet. I always feel encouraged by Peter's relationship with Jesus. He trusts Jesus enough, feels secure enough with him to ask questions, knowing he won't be ridiculed.

How do you relate to Jesus? Do you feel free to ask questions and admit that you don't understand when life is throwing up unexpected events and problems? Any healthy relationship requires honesty, and our relationship with Jesus is no exception – he knows our deepest thoughts anyway. It's as we wrestle with issues in our lives and open ourselves up to him that Jesus is able to reveal himself to us more fully and meet us in the struggle.

Lord, thank you that you know me fully, love me totally and long for me to be honest and open with you.

DEBBIE ORRISS

Water for sacrifice

After [Jesus] had washed [his disciples'] feet, had put on his robe, and had returned to the table, he said to them, 'Do you know what I have done to you? You call me Teacher and Lord – and you are right, for that is what I am. So if I, your Lord and Teacher, have washed your feet, you also ought to wash one another's feet. For I have set you an example, that you also should do as I have done to you. Very truly, I tell you, servants are not greater than their master, nor are messengers greater than the one who sent them. If you know these things, you are blessed if you do them.'

One of the most moving parts of the ordination service in Salisbury Cathedral is when the bishops kneel at the feet of the new deacons and wash their feet. Amid all the pomp and ritual of this beautiful service is a simple reminder of the calling that each of us share – to follow our Lord's example of loving service.

But what does this actually mean? Jesus tells the disciples that he is setting them an example, and his act of washing their feet, for it to have any significance, has to be taken in the context of the rest of their experience of him. If Jesus had led a life of selfish indulgence – taking power by force and trampling those around him – the act would have meant nothing. But what they have experienced is a life lived fully, with times of celebration and fun, but also lived for the benefit of others. We have seen through previous reflections how Jesus took time with people, treating them as individuals, and met their individual needs. And of course we look back on this act from the other side of the crucifixion – his ultimate act of love and self-giving for each one of us. His call to each of us is a call to love, to serve and to forgive.

Lord, I am humbled that you, the Son of God, sitting at the right hand of God the Father, entered into this world to love, to serve and to forgive. Help me to live in this way also, by the power of your Holy Spirit.

DEBBIE ORRISS

Water for life

But when they came to Jesus and saw that he was already dead, they did not break his legs. Instead, one of the soldiers pierced his side with a spear, and at once blood and water came out. (He who saw this has testified so that you also may believe. His testimony is true, and he knows that he tells the truth.) These things occurred so that the scripture might be fulfilled, 'None of his bones shall be broken.' And again another passage of scripture says, 'They will look on the one whom they have pierced.'

This, the last passage in our series on water in John, is perhaps the most moving and powerful of all. Jesus has been crucified, one of the cruellest forms of torture and tools of death. The soldiers have come to break Jesus' legs, to hasten the end of life. Without the use of their legs, someone who has been nailed to a cross cannot raise themselves up to get air into their lungs and they suffocate.

Seeing that Jesus is already dead, the soldier instead stabs him with a spear – just to make sure – and blood and water flow out. For John this is incredibly significant, and perhaps encapsulates much of what the previous reflections have considered. The water coming from Jesus' side is a sign of hope, with water again symbolising the Spirit. As Jesus told his disciples, he had to die in order for the Spirit to come, so this event speaks to us of Jesus' promises of forgiveness and cleansing, life in abundance, and daily refreshment.

My hope for us all is that we can continue to be open to the Spirit, risky as it may feel at times. In this way, Jesus can enable us to draw closer to him and receive from him all that he longs to give us for our life with him and with others. May we be agents of life-giving change as we share the good news of the gospel in our words and our actions, empowered and enlivened by the Spirit within us.

Lord, I'm overwhelmed by your love for me, and your desire to work with me to transform the lives of those around me. Help me and use me, I pray.

DEBBIE ORRISS

Joshua 1—7

By the time that Joshua son of Nun takes on the leadership of the people of Israel, we already have insight into his life and character. His training for the task had taken place over 40 years; Joshua was, along with Caleb, one of only two Israelites who had experienced slavery in Egypt, fled across the Red Sea, followed Moses through the wilderness and were to enter the promised land.

Joshua had become Moses' assistant at a young age, having been singled out to accompany him part of the way up Mount Sinai, where Moses received the commandments from God. He was with Moses on the descent when they saw the people worshipping the golden calf. Joshua was one of the twelve men sent to spy out the fertile land of Canaan. He returned with a faith-filled positive report, while all the others, save Caleb, focused on their fear of powerful enemies and fortified cities, infecting the people of Israel with their negativity.

Joshua had proved himself as a soldier and military strategist. However, he had learned that ultimately it was God who gave the victory, for his success in overcoming the Amalekites had depended on Moses' arms being lifted to God in intercession.

Joshua had observed the Israelites' fickleness, heard their complaints and seen trouble and conflict. He had witnessed God's miraculous provision, interventions and judgements. He had watched Moses' loving commitment to the people despite the frustrations of leading them. Joshua had been privileged to enter the tent of meeting with Moses, waiting there while Moses communed with God. God had instructed Moses to publicly commission Joshua as the next leader through the laying on of hands. Joshua was filled with the spirit of wisdom. At last the time had come for him to lead the people under God's authority.

Like Joshua, our life experiences prepare us for the next step on our journey. The preparation may seem lengthy! Like Joshua, we need to walk closely with God and know the Spirit's filling. The first seven chapters of Joshua give us insight into God's relationship with both individuals and groups, providing us with the wisdom to live courageously because of our confidence in God.

FIONA STRATTA

The long wait is over

After the death of Moses the Lord's servant, the Lord spoke to Joshua son of Nun, Moses' assistant… 'The time has come for you to lead these people, the Israelites, across the Jordan River into the land I am giving them. I promise you what I promised Moses… No one will be able to stand against you as long as you live. For I will be with you as I was with Moses. I will not fail you or abandon you.'

Joshua has been given the task of conquering the promised land and sharing it between the Israelite tribes. Under Moses' leadership, he experienced the taking of the territories east of the Jordan, and he has been promised that God will do the same west of the river. However, Moses is no longer there to lead. Amid his inevitable grief, Joshua must discern God's timing, direct the people and inspire them to trust God. The 40-year wait is over. He has the wonderful promise spoken to Moses before his death to hold on to: 'The Lord your God will fight for you' (Deuteronomy 3:22, NLT). He has learned that his strength does not lie in his own expertise but in the Lord. Now they are to cross the Jordan. Like Moses when he reached the Red Sea, Joshua faces a seemingly impassable stretch of water – a problem to which there is no human solution. However, he has the memory of the miraculous crossing of the Red Sea to encourage him.

We, like Joshua, may have waited many years in the hope of seeing the fulfilment of a promise or an answer to prayer. We may still be waiting. Or there may be ahead of us a Jordan to cross, a problem beyond our human reasoning and ability to solve. God's past faithfulness both in history and in our personal stories gives us confidence to persevere.

Lord, thank you that you go before us and will fight for us.
Your grace is sufficient for our needs and your strength is
demonstrated in our weakness. As we wait, thank you that
you are forming your character within us. Amen

FIONA STRATTA

The most important thing

'Be strong and courageous, for you are the one who will lead these people... Be strong and very courageous. Be careful to obey all the instructions Moses gave you. Do not deviate from them, turning either to the right or to the left. Then you will be successful in everything you do. Study this Book of Instruction continually. Meditate on it day and night so you will be sure to obey everything written in it... This is my command – be strong and courageous. Do not be afraid or discouraged. For the Lord your God is with you wherever you go.'

In these verses, God instructs Joshua that, to quote an old German proverb, 'the most important thing is that the most important thing remains the most important thing'. In order to succeed in leading the people, Joshua is to prioritise his relationship with God and follow him wholeheartedly. He is to obey diligently all the instructions (laws) given by God through Moses. To do this he needs to both study (learn) the laws and meditate on (deliberate on) them at every opportunity, day and night, so that they become embedded within him. The recall of the instructions is to bear fruit, leading to a steady, faith-filled attitude. Moreover, Joshua must take care not to compromise (turn to the left or right). God repeatedly tells him to be strong and courageous, never giving in to fear or discouragement.

The more we are consciously wholehearted in our faith journeys, the less we subconsciously slip into being half-hearted – the two are incompatible. Our top priority is to keep our top priority as our top priority. It is not just a matter of reading, or even rote-learning, promises, verses or passages from God's word, but of meditating on them, so that the roots go deep within us, gradually transforming us. This is key in unlearning our human knee-jerk reaction of fear and discouragement, and establishing a default position of trust in the sovereign God, so that we can stay grounded and secure in his love.

Joshua learned from Moses that God is slow to anger, abounding in love, compassionate, faithful, gracious and forgiving. What an incentive to spend time with him!

FIONA STRATTA

Being community

Joshua then commanded the officers of Israel, 'Go through the camp and tell the people to get their provisions ready. In three days you will cross the Jordan River and take possession of the land the Lord your God is giving you.' Then Joshua called together the tribes of Reuben, Gad, and the half-tribe of Manasseh. He told them... 'Your wives, children, and livestock may remain here in the land Moses assigned to you on the east side of the Jordan River. But your strong warriors, fully armed, must lead the other tribes across the Jordan to help them conquer their territory. Stay with them until the Lord gives them rest, as he has given you rest.'

Joshua gives the leaders God's instructions and then addresses a situation that arose under Moses' leadership. The tribes of Reuben, Gad and the half-tribe of Manasseh had asked Moses to allow them to settle east of the River Jordan, where there was excellent pastureland for their flocks. Moses decided that they could do so, but first they had to commit themselves to conquering the promised land for the sake of the other tribes. They were not to enjoy rest, freedom and prosperity while their fellow Israelites were fighting for the same privileges.

There is a challenge here not just to look to our own interests but also to the interests of others. The episode with these tribes reminds us that we are to love our neighbours as ourselves. In Jesus' parable of the good Samaritan, we recall that our neighbours are those God brings to our attention whose needs we can alleviate in small or larger ways. They may be geographically near or far, but we cannot rest 'east of the Jordan' in plenty and unconcern while others are facing battles in their lives. It challenges our complacency in enjoying freedom and a way of life that may well come at the expense of others who need our help.

Lord, we have limited resources and limited energies. May your Spirit place on our hearts those people and situations where we can make a difference, for your name's sake. Amen

FIONA STRATTA

Follow the leader, encourage the leader

[The tribes] answered Joshua, 'We will do whatever you command us, and we will go wherever you send us. We will obey you just as we obeyed Moses. And may the Lord your God be with you as he was with Moses. Anyone who rebels against your orders and does not obey your words and everything you command will be put to death. So be strong and courageous!' Then Joshua secretly sent out two spies from the Israelite camp... He instructed them, 'Scout out the land on the other side of the Jordan River, especially around Jericho.'

The tribes listen and promise to stick to their agreement with Moses. They verbalise their commitment, which will not be without its dangers and inconveniences. However, they go further than this, encouraging Joshua to be 'strong and courageous', using the very words that Joshua has received from the Lord.

How uplifting it must be for Joshua to hear those words again, this time from those he is leading! It seems that these words encourage him to send two spies across the Jordan, 40 years after he went on a similar mission. Unlike the twelve that Moses sent, Joshua chooses only two trusted men for this task. Perhaps he felt that two men could stay undercover more easily. Also his experience taught him that two men were more likely to agree over their report than twelve. Although God has promised Joshua the land, he still feels the need to send out scouts. Perhaps this was a prompt from the 'spirit of wisdom', for their assignment was to play a crucial role in God's masterplan for salvation.

We can be reluctant and reticent followers or, like the three tribes, enthusiastic and encouraging ones. What a difference it makes to our leaders if we affirm them and their aspirations! It is heartening for them to know that others are faithfully committed, even when there is a potential cost or sacrifice involved. Our leaders are human and therefore vulnerable to discouragement. We can take opportunities to encourage them to trust in our dependable God and to be strong enough to take bold steps of faith.

How can we be proactive in affirming and encouraging our leaders?

FIONA STRATTA

Help from unexpected quarters

Rahab had hidden the two men... Before the spies went to sleep that night, Rahab went up on the roof to talk with them. 'I know the Lord has given you this land... We are all afraid of you... For we have heard how the Lord made a dry path for you through the Red Sea... No wonder our hearts have melted in fear! No one has the courage to fight after hearing such things. For the Lord your God is the supreme God of the heavens above and the earth below.'

Joshua saw it as a wise military decision to get a feel for his enemy by sending out scouts. At this stage God has not told him how the city will be taken, and Joshua would have been considering the typical warfare strategies of his time. The spies' entry into Jericho did not go unnoticed, but they find unexpected support in Rahab, a prostitute whose home is within the city walls. She hides the spies from the king's men under flax on the roof of her house. Rahab gives them protection, advice and the exact encouragement that they need: the people of Jericho know of the Israelites' reputation and are petrified. She then does something extraordinary – she confesses her faith in their God. The spies could act with cynicism, but they show shrewd trust.

Becoming a part of the people of God was possible through a confession of faith; it was not a privilege for only the Israelites. Rahab and her family are to be saved if they demonstrate their faith by obeying the spies' instructions. God has purposes for her – Rahab's name is found in the lineage of Jesus in Matthew 1.

We, too, can be blessed and receive friendship, advice and help from surprising quarters and people as we live in faithful obedience, open to God and to others. God can speak to us through unexpected words from unexpected people. This episode is also a call not to overlook anyone and the part they may play in God's kingdom purposes.

Lord, may we be ready to be blessed and give blessings to others in unforeseen situations and ways. May we hear your voice when and where we least expect it. Amen

FIONA STRATTA

Dry ground

The Lord told Joshua, 'Today I will begin to make you a great leader in the eyes of all the Israelites... Give this command to the priests who carry the Ark of the Covenant: "When you reach the banks of the Jordan River, take a few steps into the river and stop there."'... So the people left their camp to cross the Jordan, and the priests who were carrying the Ark of the Covenant went ahead of them. It was the harvest season, and the Jordan was overflowing its banks. But as soon as the feet of the priests who were carrying the Ark touched the water at the river's edge, the water above that point began backing up a great distance away... And the water below that point flowed on to the Dead Sea until the riverbed was dry. Then all the people crossed over near the town of Jericho.

At last the instructions become more specific – the land has been promised and the time for action has come. Interestingly, Joshua is not given all the details by God, just the instruction that the priests should take a few steps into the river. Joshua's experience of the Red Sea crossing enables him to realise what God is about to do. His faith in this leads him to explain to the Israelites what will happen. He is asking this next generation, none of whom (save Caleb) experienced the escape from Egypt, to demonstrate their individual and corporate faith by following the Ark of the Covenant, the symbol of God's presence. Miraculously the water backs up. Even if this is a natural event, such as a mudslide upstream, God's timing is perfect. The people cross on dry ground.

We may be inspired reading of the faith stories, revivals and miracles experienced by previous generations, but the challenge remains for *us* to act when God prompts and see him working in *our* lives. Sometimes it may seem less daunting to stay in the known wilderness than to step out towards an unknown, hoped-for 'land of plenty'.

Better a journey on dry ground across and into the unknown
than staying on the bank afraid to go forward.

FIONA STRATTA

A permanent memorial and message

So Joshua called together the twelve men he had chosen – one from each of the tribes of Israel. He told them, 'Go into the middle of the Jordan, in front of the Ark of the Lord your God. Each of you must pick up one stone and carry it out on your shoulder... We will use these stones to build a memorial. In the future your children will ask you, "What do these stones mean?" Then you can tell them, "They remind us that the Jordan River stopped flowing when the Ark of the Lord's Covenant went across." These stones will stand as a memorial among the people of Israel forever.'

How could anyone ever forget the events of that day: seeing the river run dry as the priests entered it carrying the Ark of the Covenant, watching thousands upon thousands of people crossing the dry river bed? Joshua, however, had experienced how the Israelites' praise and worship turned quickly to complaint. He knows the importance of consciously remembering what the Lord has done for them, so God's instructions strike a chord. Those who crossed the Jordan are to use the stones not only as an opportunity to tell their children about what happened on that day, but also as a reminder of its significance. This is twofold: first, it demonstrated the power of the Lord to all the nations of the world; second, it was a sign to the Israelites so that they 'might fear the Lord [their] God forever' (v. 24, NLT).

We might have 'memorials' – objects, photos, certificates or pictures – that are reminders of God's work in our lives, his presence and his power. These are important in stoking our faith and also act as a stimulus to respect and hold in awe our God (to 'fear' the Lord). Like the stones, these remind us that our successes, joys and deliverance are the result of God's gracious care, protection and provision. They teach us humility.

God made Joshua a great leader that day in the eyes of all the people. However, the memorial directed the people's attention away from him and back to God. How can we use our 'memorials' to point ourselves and others to God?

FIONA STRATTA

Vulnerability

At that time the Lord told Joshua, 'Make flint knives and circumcise this second generation of Israelites.'... Those who left Egypt had all been circumcised, but none of those born after the Exodus, during the years in the wilderness, had been circumcised... After all the males had been circumcised, they rested in the camp until they were healed. Then the Lord said to Joshua, 'Today I have rolled away the shame of your slavery in Egypt.' So that place has been called Gilgal to this day.

Joshua's instructions from God are astonishing, for it will leave the Israelites weak and vulnerable to enemy attack. From a human perspective, surely this task should have been done on the other side of the river, in relative safety. But God sees the big picture: he knows that the Israelites will have time to heal, because the people groups west of the Jordan have 'lost heart' and are 'paralysed with fear' (Joshua 5:1, NLT).

God requires that the second generation of males be circumcised to reaffirm his covenant with Abraham. He has promised the land and their response is commitment, demonstrated in circumcision. Having miraculously crossed the Jordan, the people are full of confidence in God. God's timing for the circumcisions is perfect, for now this generation has seen what only Caleb and Joshua had previously witnessed – the parting of the water. Now they are prepared to follow wholeheartedly, realising that a makeshift camp with God is safer than a fortified city without him.

The name 'Gilgal' sounds like the Hebrew for roll. Maybe the 'shame' to be rolled away was that of the previous generation who had disobeyed God. Or perhaps it was the 'shame' of being scorned by other people groups as an unsuccessful, previously enslaved, nomadic people of seemingly little consequence.

At times we can feel vulnerable following the Lord. His ways and challenges can sometimes seem unwise from a human perspective. We can remember that God sees the big picture.

This episode foreshadows a greater 'rolling away' –
that of the stone to the tomb at the resurrection of Jesus,
who through his death took away our shame.

FIONA STRATTA

A land flowing with milk and honey

While the Israelites were camped at Gilgal on the plains of Jericho, they celebrated Passover on the evening of the fourteenth day of the first month. The very next day they began to eat unleavened bread and roasted grain harvested from the land. No manna appeared on the day they first ate from the crops of the land, and it was never seen again. So from that time on the Israelites ate from the crops of Canaan.

It is time for the Israelites – humbled, aware of God's strength and their weakness – to reflect and worship. At long last they can celebrate God's goodness by commemorating the Passover meal. Joshua takes seriously the command to remember and obey the laws that God gave to Moses. His focus is on being true to God first and foremost and encouraging others to be the same.

The land that the Israelites have entered is rich in milk and yoghurt from goats and sheep, and with honey and syrup from bees, figs and grapes. No doubt they savour the variety of tastes that they are now enjoying west of the Jordan, but no longer can they rely on the daily collection of manna. Are they shocked that first day on which no manna appears? God had provided them with a supernatural supply all the time that it had been needed. Now he will continue to provide for them through the harvests in Canaan, but they will need to work the land.

Perhaps we have personally experienced times when God has provided for us in amazing ways. Very often God's provision and our work go hand in hand: his provision is our work. As we pray for our 'daily bread', we rejoice and recognise God's generous heart in meeting both big and small needs.

Thank you, Lord, that you have instructed us not to worry about food, drink and clothes, or to let such concerns dominate our thoughts. May we increasingly learn to relax and rest in you as we more confidently trust you. Help us to seek first your kingdom and live God-centred lives, celebrating your goodness and trusting that you will meet our needs. Amen (Based on verses from Matthew 6.)

FIONA STRATTA

The commander of the Lord's army

When Joshua was near the town of Jericho, he looked up and saw a man standing in front of him with sword in hand. Joshua went up to him and demanded, 'Are you friend or foe?' 'Neither one,' he replied. 'I am the commander of the Lord's army.' At this, Joshua fell with his face to the ground in reverence. 'I am at your command,' Joshua said. 'What do you want your servant to do?' The commander of the Lord's army replied, 'Take off your sandals, for the place where you are standing is holy.' And Joshua did as he was told.

After the Passover meal, Joshua went to look at Jericho for himself. Maybe he was wondering when and how they should proceed. How could they attack such a strongly fortified city? Could they besiege a place containing such ample supplies? His brave challenge to an armed stranger brings the answers. Joshua, God's chosen leader, a man of considerable authority, finds himself face-to-face with the commander of the Lord's army. Joshua recognises that before such a being he is but a servant under authority; he falls to the ground in awe.

Joshua's humility is striking. Like Moses in Exodus 3, he is told to take off his sandals for he is standing on holy ground. Moses was once a prince; Joshua was once a slave. Moses covered his face; Joshua falls down, his face to the ground. Moses put up a fight, he 'protested to God' (Exodus 3:11, NLT); Joshua says, 'I am at your command. What do you want your servant to do?'

Joshua initially thinks that he is face-to-face with a foe or one of his own men. The reality is that something spiritual is happening, something colossal: Joshua is about to be clay in the potter's hands. Israel's commander is in his turn being commanded by the commander of the Lord's army. Joshua will be key in bringing about the next part of God's restoration plan for the Israelites.

Lord, help us to recognise the spiritual battles taking place around us.
May we have the humility to fight them by unreservedly
depending on you and your methods. Amen

FIONA STRATTA

Already given

But the Lord said to Joshua, 'I have given you Jericho, its king, and all its strong warriors. You and your fighting men should march around the town once a day for six days. Seven priests will walk ahead of the Ark, each carrying a ram's horn. On the seventh day you are to march around the town seven times, with the priests blowing the horns. When you hear the priests give one long blast on the rams' horns, have all the people shout as loud as they can. Then the walls of the town will collapse, and the people can charge straight into the town.'

Finally the instructions are given and Joshua can prepare the people. These words could be a continuation of the instructions given by the commander of the Lord's army. Joshua is told that he has been given Jericho – note the sense of completion. Jericho has been promised to the Israelites but they have to take action to receive it. God's promises are to be claimed and acted upon. He has given so much: forgiveness and freedom through his Son; the Holy Spirit to teach, guide and comfort us; the fruit and gifts of the Spirit; 'every spiritual blessing in the heavenly realms' (Ephesians 1:3, NLT).

God revealed his plan to Joshua one stage at a time: first the crossing of the Jordan, then circumcision, next Passover and finally the means of taking Jericho. God gave Moses the promise of a spacious and fertile land when he met with him at the burning bush (Exodus 3). The people needed to hold on to that vision during their wilderness days. The working out of the promise became clear only gradually, according to God's wisdom. The Israelites would not have been ready for the extraordinary instructions concerning Jericho before they had experienced the miraculous crossing of the Jordan, the humbling of their bodies and souls, and the renewal of their faith through the Passover meal. God often reveals each stage of our journey little by little. We need to hang on to his vision for us – to make us more like his Son Jesus Christ.

Lord, help us to trust your infinite wisdom.
Give us courage to act on your promises.

FIONA STRATTA

So the Lord was with Joshua

The men who had been spies went in and brought out Rahab... They moved her whole family to a safe place near the camp of Israel. Then the Israelites burned the town and everything in it. Only the things made from silver, gold, bronze, or iron were kept for the treasury of the Lord's house. So Joshua spared Rahab the prostitute and her relatives who were with her in the house, because she had hidden the spies Joshua sent to Jericho. And she lives among the Israelites to this day... So the Lord was with Joshua and his reputation spread throughout the land.

Such is the Israelites' level of faith in God and trust in Joshua's leadership that they are willing to obey the most unusual battle instructions they have ever received – and the walls come tumbling down. This unique event in history is accompanied by the instructions to devote everything to God through its destruction, save the valuables to be put aside – not for personal gain but for God's purposes (vv. 17–19). Such instructions are not given at future battles, but on this occasion God in his sovereignty deems it necessary to judge the city for its corrupt practices and to prevent defilement of his people. Nevertheless, Rahab and her family, because of their faith in the living God, are rescued.

Often evil regimes and practices implode and destroy themselves. However, there are times of divine judgement, and this is one such example. Rather like in the narrative of the destruction of Sodom and Gomorrah, when Lot and his family escape God's wrath, God reaches out in mercy to those in Jericho who acknowledge him.

To start with, Rahab and her family were outside the camp, presumably while they were ritually unclean. Then they lived fruitfully 'among' the people. Such is God's grace. A fresh start takes dramatic pruning, but God is the gardener who prunes in order that we become more fruitful.

'Apart from me you can do nothing' (John 15:5, NLT). Are there 'walls' in our lives that it seems we cannot penetrate? Like Joshua, we can await God's timing and methods, ready to take action and cooperate while he brings the walls tumbling down.

FIONA STRATTA

Honest prayer

Then Joshua cried out, 'Oh, Sovereign Lord, why did you bring us across the Jordan River if you are going to let the Amorites kill us? If only we had been content to stay on the other side! Lord, what can I say now that Israel has fled from its enemies? For when the Canaanites and all the other people living in the land hear about it, they will surround us and wipe our name off the face of the earth. And then what will happen to the honour of your great name?'

The defeat at Ai has been interpreted in different ways. One interpretation is that Joshua and the Israelites became too self-confident. There is no record of Joshua, by then 'famous all over the land' (6:27, MSG), enquiring of the Lord prior to sending the spies and before deciding, on their advice, to send a small army to attack Ai. Failure followed and the Israelites became a people whose 'courage melted away' (7:5, NLT).

Joshua at this stage has no knowledge that the Lord's instructions have been violated. His honest and desperate prayer demonstrates that leaders are not immune to losing courage and dreading the worst. His fear is that the people he is leading will be wiped out by their surrounding enemies. However, his concern is not only for the Israelites, but also for the honour of God's name. His prayer receives a surprising answer: the root of the failure to take Ai was the result of moral failure within the camp of Israel. No wonder the writer of Proverbs penned the words 'Above all else, guard your heart, for everything you do flows from it' (4:23, NIV).

Our experiences shape our level of confidence. This episode shows us that, however confident we feel, each new circumstance in life, whether large or small, needs to be faced with humility and dependence on God. We sometimes end prayers with the words 'for your name's sake' or 'to the glory of your name'. Saying these words with sincerity focuses our attention on seeking the Lord's honour in all things.

May we guard our hearts and approach you honestly, for your glory, honour and name's sake. Amen

FIONA STRATTA

Purify my heart

'Get up! Command the people to purify themselves in preparation for tomorrow. For this is what the Lord, the God of Israel, says: Hidden among you, O Israel, are things set apart for the Lord. You will never defeat your enemies until you remove these things from among you.'... They piled a great heap of stones over Achan, which remains to this day. That is why the place has been called the Valley of Trouble ever since. So the Lord was no longer angry.

Achan stole and hid some objects of great worth that had been dedicated to the Lord. We do not know whether his family were privy to this. The stoning (v. 25b) must have been a terrible event, and the new pile of stones placed over Achan's body a grave warning that God cannot be fooled. This is a critical time in history, and purity of heart and purpose is essential to the future of the Israelites. The action of one man affected them all, for they were a covenant community. This dark episode takes place in the Valley of Achor, meaning trouble. Maybe the early believers were reminded of this event when Ananias and Sapphira died following their deceit (Acts 5).

Rebellion against God has consequences. Our negative or selfish attitudes, words and actions affect not only those we love, work and live with, but also our spiritual communities. No wonder we are warned to protect our fellowships from moral failure. Both God's honour and our witness to those around us are at stake.

We read of these key historical judgements, but awesomely we discover in the Bible a God of grace and restoration who 'does not deal harshly with us, as we deserve' (Psalm 103:10, NLT). This series ends on a note of hope – Joshua once again listens to God, who gives him encouragement (Joshua 8:1). We also know and rejoice in the promises made to future generations: the Valley of Achor will become a resting place and a door of hope (Isaiah 65:10; Hosea 2:15).

Lord, purify our hearts. Thank you for your grace and mercy.
Make the 'Valleys of Achor' in our lives places where we can
eventually find rest, hope and restoration. Amen

FIONA STRATTA

Humility

Have you ever looked at the stars on a dark, clear night or viewed the landscape from a mountaintop and felt very small? When we measure ourselves against the scale of God's creation, it's easy to feel insignificant. Yet we too – amazingly – are part of that creation, and are loved so much that God chose to live and die for us in the person of Jesus Christ.

Psalm 8:3–4 (NRSV) describes that sense of astonishment: 'When I look at your heavens, the work of your fingers, the moon and the stars that you have established; what are human beings that you are mindful of them, mortals that you care for them?' The psalmist goes on to praise the fact that we are made only 'a little lower than God' (v.5, NRSV). It is a hymn of thanksgiving, measuring humanity against the boundless possibilities of God and rejoicing in divine generosity.

There is a significant difference between expressing awe in God's presence and abasing ourselves in response to God's power. The first reaction responds respectfully to God's greatness, while the second suggests fear and insecurity. Similarly, there is a significant gulf between genuine humility before God – the knowledge that all we are and all we can achieve are due solely to God's generosity – and the falsely unctuous self-effacement that tries to gather attention and reward: 'Look how humble I am!' Jesus recognised this, always responding with kindness to people who were reluctant to bother him with their needs and warning against the self-delusion that insists, 'Lord, I thank you that I am better than that person.'

Humility is one of the traditional Christian virtues, often thought of as the opposite of the deadly sin of pride. But how we understand humility, and how we acquire it, is a developing theme through scripture. For many characters in the Old Testament, humility is something that has to be learned, often through painful experience. Both individuals and entire nations gradually come to recognise God as the source of all greatness, rather than their own efforts. Then, in the New Testament, Jesus appears and offers us a new way to live: leading through servanthood and loving even our enemies. Christ is the exemplar of absolute humility through complete openness to God.

AMANDA BLOOR

'Who told you?'

The Lord God called to the man, and said to him, 'Where are you?' He said, 'I heard the sound of you in the garden, and I was afraid, because I was naked; and I hid myself.' He said, 'Who told you that you were naked? Have you eaten from the tree of which I commanded you not to eat?'

It is shame, rather than humility, that causes Adam and Eve to hide themselves from God's gaze. Having eaten from the tree of the knowledge of good and evil, they realise that they are unclothed and attempt to hide themselves among the trees of the garden. Their actions are, of course, revealing in more ways than one: God sees not just their nakedness, but also their uncomfortable awareness that they have done wrong. They have taken a step which has changed them for ever.

Expelled from paradise, where they had existed in childlike innocence, the man and woman have to live as adults whose actions have consequences. Now they suffer the pains and indignities of everyday life: hard work, danger, physical exhaustion, the limitations of the physical body. They learn humility through their experiences and their failures, through parenthood, thankfulness and sorrow. They learn, in short, to be human.

God's question to them, 'Who told you?', is a moment of painful clarity. Adam and Eve are forced to face their weaknesses and limitations. Instead of becoming 'like God', as the serpent promised, they discover that they are merely a man and a woman deceived, misled, reliant upon each other and thrown upon God's mercy. Most of us will have faced a similar realisation. We too need the humility to acknowledge our own frailties and mistakes, that we may not trust in ourselves alone but depend instead upon the generous strength of our creator.

God our creator, may we listen to your voice rather than the beguiling promises of the world. Help us to be steadfast in faith and trust. Walk with us as we travel through life, and grant us the gift of humility so that we may choose to be guided and led always by you.

AMANDA BLOOR

'It is the Lord your God'

Joshua summoned all Israel, their elders and heads, their judges and officers, and said to them, 'I am now old and well advanced in years; and you have seen all that the Lord your God has done to all these nations for your sake, for it is the Lord your God who has fought for you… hold fast to the Lord your God, as you have done to this day. For the Lord has driven out before you great and strong nations.'

Joshua was commissioned to carry on the task begun by Moses. 'Be strong and courageous,' ordered God, 'for the Lord your God is with you wherever you go' (1:9, NRSV). Joshua believed God's promise and became a skilled military leader. He sent spies out to gather intelligence, and like Moses dried up raging waters so that his people could cross the Jordan on dry ground. With the sound of trumpets, Joshua broke down the walls of Jericho and took control of the city. He maintained discipline within his army, and relentlessly hunted down his enemies until 'the whole land' (11:23, NRSV) belonged to Israel and there could be rest.

We see all too often in our own time the corrupting effects of power. Whether manifesting itself in abusive behaviour or arrogance, there is danger in believing that we deserve adulation and respect. Success against all the odds can lead us to think that we are invincible. We can begin to think of ourselves as the centre of our world.

Joshua avoids falling into this trap. Now an old man, he reminds his people that everything they have achieved has been with God's help. He urges them to remain faithful and to love God, following the commandments and keeping the covenant. Joshua's humility allows him to appreciate his part in responding to God's calling, but at the same time to recognise that without God, his success would not have been possible. It is humility that makes him a great leader.

Are you able to look at your achievements with pleasure, while recognising God's guiding hand upon your life? Humility can lead us into partnership with the God who longs to help us fulfil our potential and whose strength is greater than our imaginings.

AMANDA BLOOR

Trust me, I'm a prophet

Barak said to [Deborah], 'If you will go with me, I will go; but if you will not go with me, I will not go.' And she said, 'I will surely go with you; nevertheless, the road on which you are going will not lead to your glory, for the Lord will sell Sisera into the hand of a woman.' Then Deborah got up and went with Barak to Kedesh.

Deborah is one of the few female leaders to be mentioned by name in the Old Testament. She is described as a 'prophetess' whose wisdom enables her to be a significant figure among the Israelites. A woman of influence, she acts as judge, arbitrating between individuals and offering advice to the community, and she is unafraid to summon Barak, a military commander, into her presence.

Although Deborah assures him that if he follows her instructions, God will enable them to defeat the Canaanite army, Barak is reluctant to take strategic direction from a civilian and a woman. 'I will only do this if you have the courage of your convictions,' he tells her. 'If you're prepared to come into battle alongside me, then I'll trust you.'

How would you react to a barely veiled insult like this, I wonder? Deborah could have responded with anger, but instead there's a hint of amusement. She agrees to Barak's terms, but she points out that when the battle is won, it won't be seen as his victory, but that of a woman. Her words are truer than Barak could have imagined: not only does the battle go as she says, but Sisera, the enemy commander, is killed by another woman, Jael, the wife of a clan chief.

It is not only the Canaanites who are subdued that day. Barak, the leader of 10,000 men, has recognised that even he has fears and weaknesses. And he's had to learn the humility that comes after a blow to one's pride. God's guiding hand can equip anyone (even a woman!) to do great things.

Give me the humility, Lord, to listen to you through the voices of others, and make me ready to follow wherever you lead.

AMANDA BLOOR

71

'Do not hide it from me'

Eli called Samuel and said, 'Samuel, my son.' He said, 'Here I am.' Eli said, 'What was it that he told you? Do not hide it from me. May God do so to you and more also, if you hide anything from me of all that he told you.' So Samuel told him everything and hid nothing from him. Then he said, 'It is the Lord; let him do what seems good to him.'

Have you ever had to give bad news to someone close to you? It can be hard to hurt someone we care about; harder still if we are implying that they have played a part in their own misfortune. This is the position in which Samuel finds himself. Still a child, woken from sleep by God's insistent calling, he is tasked with delivering a difficult message to Eli the priest. God has already warned the old man that his sons are corrupt and sinful, but Eli has not disciplined them. Now the very office of priesthood has been dishonoured by association, and God has had enough. 'This must stop,' says God. 'It is too late to offer sacrifices and regrets.'

Samuel lies awake for the rest of the night, afraid to tell Eli that his sons are to die and his family line is to come abruptly to an end. Yet Eli knows that God has spoken to the boy and recognises Samuel's discomfort. 'Tell me it all,' he demands.

We can imagine the conversation, followed perhaps by a silence as Eli takes in the enormity of God's message. Doubly humbled, by the recognition that he has been overindulgent of his sons' behaviour, and by the knowledge that God now speaks to the boy who is his apprentice, he might have responded with anger or bluster. Instead, Eli shows – at last! – the humility that comes from acceptance of human weakness and divine righteousness. 'It is the Lord,' he says, 'let him do what seems good.'

Can we, I wonder, find the humility to face our failures and listen to what is painful to hear? God tries again and again to call us back to a right way of living whenever we go astray.

AMANDA BLOOR

'Whom shall I send?'

I said: 'Woe is me! I am lost, for I am a man of unclean lips, and I live among a people of unclean lips; yet my eyes have seen the King, the Lord of hosts!' Then one of the seraphs flew to me, holding a live coal that had been taken from the altar with a pair of tongs. The seraph touched my mouth with it and said: 'Now that this has touched your lips, your guilt has departed and your sin is blotted out.'

Humility before God can sometimes lead to paralysis. Here we see Isaiah, the prophet and visionary, describing his encounter with God and his terrified response. Aware of his failings and those of his community, Isaiah trembles with recognition of his insignificance before the awesome might of the Lord. 'I am lost!' he cries.

Yet God has granted this vision for a purpose and has plans for Isaiah. Straight away, a seraph acts to both reassure and energise the prophet. By touching his lips with a live coal from the altar, the seraph is symbolically cleansing Isaiah's mouth with fire – his lips are no longer 'unclean' – and offering him a new start. 'Your guilt has departed,' he is told.

Isaiah, released from his fears, is immediately eager to serve God in whatever way he can. 'Whom shall I send?' asks God, and Isaiah, with bouncy enthusiasm, is able to respond, 'Here I am; send me!' (v.8, NRSV).

It's good to retain a sense of humility when approaching God's presence. But the humility of awe and wonder needs to be balanced with the humility to trust that God is loving and powerful and good. If God calls us into service, or offers us a glimpse of the divine presence, then God will also equip us to respond appropriately. How many times, I wonder, have we mused, 'Does God want me to do this?', only to think, 'Surely, not me.' Humility is not an excuse for inaction.

Gracious God, you offer to equip us with all we need to follow and serve you. Help me to have the humility to open myself to you, accepting your gifts. Let me say in eager thanksgiving, 'Here I am; send me!'

AMANDA BLOOR

Should I not be concerned?

The people of Nineveh believed God; they proclaimed a fast, and everyone, great and small, put on sackcloth. When the news reached the king of Nineveh, he rose from his throne, removed his robe, covered himself with sackcloth, and sat in ashes… When God saw what they did, how they turned from their evil ways, God changed his mind about the calamity that he had said he would bring upon them; and he did not do it.

You might think that Jonah, after being saved from the belly of the whale, would have appreciated God's readiness to forgive those who ask for rescue. Yet when God asks him a second time to go to the city of Nineveh and issue a warning against the wickedness practised there, Jonah remains reluctant. We have the impression that he has learned that resistance to God's command is unwise – running away the first time led him to be thrown off a storm-tossed ship and swallowed by a 'large fish' – but he is still angry at the task given to him.

Jonah walks to the centre of the city and prophesies that in 40 days, Nineveh will be overthrown. The people are appalled, and all of them, from the greatest to the least, go into mourning. In humbleness they sit in sackcloth and ashes, fasting as a sign of their repentance and crying to God for forgiveness. Even the king abases himself before God.

The genuine humility shown by the citizens of Nineveh is their salvation. But Jonah is furious, feeling that he has been made to look a fool. Sitting under the shade of a bush, he sulks in the heat of the sun. 'I knew that you would relent,' he complains. 'I might as well be dead.' 'Should I not be concerned?' God replies. 'You care about this bush, which you did not plant – I care about the 120,000 people of Nineveh.' The behaviour of the 'wicked' people of Nineveh contrasts with Jonah's self-absorption. Perhaps he too learned, eventually, to be humble before God.

Give me ears to hear your calling, Lord, and a heart that is willing to respond. Help me to put others' needs first, rather than my own dignity.

AMANDA BLOOR

Where is the king?

Wise men from the East came to Jerusalem, asking, 'Where is the child who has been born king of the Jews? For we observed his star at its rising, and have come to pay him homage. When King Herod heard this, he was frightened, and all Jerusalem with him; and calling together all the chief priests and scribes of the people, he inquired of them where the Messiah was to be born.

It must be exhausting to be insecure of your position, knowing that your power can be taken away at any moment. Herod rules by fear – and by the permission of the Roman empire. So when visitors from far away arrive asking about the birth of a new king, he panics. He realises that they must be referring to the promised Messiah, whom he views only as a potential rival. And he is determined that he will not be usurped.

The nativity story is not all angels and starlight, but quickly becomes dark and difficult to hear. The wise men, warned in a dream not to let Herod know of the child's location, go home by a different route. Herod, infuriated by the failure of his plan and by the disobedience of the foreign visitors, massacres all the babies 'in and around Bethlehem' (v. 16, NRSV). If he cannot identify a particular child, he will kill them all.

Is this partly the fault of the wise men, who go to Herod's palace in the city instead of following the star to the small town where the child has been born? Yet where else would one expect to look for an infant king? It is hard to imagine that the 'son of David' would be found in simple surroundings, born to ordinary people, but this is how God comes among us, in quietness and humility. Riches and human power swiftly lose their appeal when measured against true treasure: the love and grace offered to us through Christ.

Lord, help me to look for your presence today. Remind me that you came to us not as a king, but as a child. Give me the humility to see beyond appearances and recognise your love for the whole of your creation – even me.

AMANDA BLOOR

You should have known!

[Jesus'] mother said to him, 'Child, why have you treated us like this? Look, your father and I have been searching for you in great anxiety.' He said to them, 'Why were you searching for me? Did you not know that I must be in my Father's house?' But they did not understand what he said to them. Then he went down with them and came to Nazareth, and was obedient to them.

Young people do not always think of the consequences of their actions. It is terrifying to lose a child in a crowd and awful to think of the dreadful things that might befall them. Imagine how distraught Mary and Joseph must have been when they realised that the twelve-year-old Jesus was not – as they had thought – journeying with friends, but had been left behind in a city full of revellers. It took them three days to find him, and their relief at his safety quickly turns to frustration at his thoughtlessness. 'How could you do this to us?' cries Mary, while Jesus, like youngsters the world over, brushes aside their concerns. 'You should have known where I'd be,' he argues. 'I need to be in my Father's house.'

It's easy to picture two emotionally and physically exhausted parents telling off a sulky young man. I suspect that Jesus was reminded of his duties to the people who were responsible for him and told that he would have to prove his reliability before being let out of their sight again. We don't know how long it took all three to calm down, but we do know this: Jesus adapts to his parents' requirements after this episode. We are told that he returns to Nazareth with Mary and Joseph and from that moment on is 'obedient to them'. Even the Son of God must listen to the parents who love him and follow their direction.

Are there times when you insist against all the evidence that you know best, or that criticism is unfair because 'they should have known'? We can all be defensive of our actions while knowing in our hearts that we could have done better. Ask for the humility to follow God's guidance.

AMANDA BLOOR

I am not he

[John] went into all the region around the Jordan, proclaiming a baptism of repentance for the forgiveness of sins… As the people were filled with expectation, and all were questioning in their hearts concerning John, whether he might be the Messiah, John answered all of them by saying, 'I baptise you with water; but one who is more powerful than I is coming; I am not worthy to untie the thong of his sandals. He will baptise you with the Holy Spirit and fire.'

It may sound obvious, but we are not Christ. No matter how hard we try to work for God, we are only human. We can only do our best, in the strength of the Holy Spirit. John the Baptist knew this very well. He was a great prophet – miraculously conceived, dedicated to God's service before his birth and driven to leave his wilderness home in order to 'prepare the way of the Lord' (Matthew 3:3, NRSV). Yet despite his holiness, John knows his limitations. He calls people to repentance, but he is clear that he is not the promised Messiah. 'I am not he,' he tells the curious crowds. 'One who is more powerful than I is coming.'

How easy it would have been for John to accept the adulation of his followers. If people tell us that we are wonderful, it's tempting to believe that this must be so. But John knew the truth about his calling and knew too that his vocation, revealed to his father by the angel Gabriel, was to 'make ready' God's people. It's possible that John knew that Jesus was the one promised; he certainly knew that he was not the one.

Humility can save us from false self-belief and keep us aware of our limitations. John's proclamations were crucial to Jesus' early ministry, and he was brave in prophecy: his witness to God's coming kingdom led to his death at the hands of Herod Antipas. But he was not the Messiah. He lived out his calling with courage and determination. That was enough.

God of all wisdom, source of our strength, help us to recognise our vocation in the world and trust in your power to help us achieve it.

AMANDA BLOOR

I am not worthy

When [a centurion] heard about Jesus, he sent some Jewish elders to him, asking him to come and heal his slave... And Jesus went with them, but when he was not far from the house, the centurion sent friends to say to him, 'Lord, do not trouble yourself, for I am not worthy to have you come under my roof; therefore I did not presume to come to you. But only speak the word, and let my servant be healed.'

This is a fascinating exchange of formalities. The centurion, concerned about his slave who is near to death, has heard of Jesus' reputation. Although part of the occupying Roman forces in Capernaum, the soldier respects the locals and their traditions; we are told that he loves the people and was responsible for building their synagogue (v. 5). So instead of approaching Jesus himself, he sends a deputation from the Jewish community on his behalf. They plead his case, affirming his worthiness, and Jesus agrees to return with them to the centurion's house.

The politeness does not end there. As Jesus approaches, the centurion sends friends to meet him, but they do not escort him into the building. They have a message: 'The centurion begs you not to trouble yourself to enter his house.' In another setting, we might wonder if the Roman did not want to be tainted by contact with an itinerant Jewish teacher, but nothing in this passage suggests anything other than humility and absolute trust. The centurion, a soldier, a commander of men, knows that when he issues an order, it will be carried out. 'If you, similarly, speak the word,' the messengers tell Jesus, 'the slave will be healed.' Jesus is amazed to find such faith from a non-Jew, a powerful Roman, and the centurion's trust is rewarded. By the time his friends return to the house, the centurion's slave is well again.

This is not false humility. The centurion knows his own worth and his own influence. But he recognises authority when he sees it, and pays it the appropriate respect.

Are we able to say humbly to Jesus, 'I am not worthy,'
yet trust that he will respond to our requests?

AMANDA BLOOR

Become like a child

The disciples came to Jesus and asked, 'Who is the greatest in the kingdom of heaven?' He called a child, whom he put among them, and said, 'Truly I tell you, unless you change and become like children, you will never enter the kingdom of heaven. Whoever becomes humble like this child is the greatest in the kingdom of heaven. Whoever welcomes one such child in my name welcomes me.'

If you have ever had dealings with small children, you will know that the conventional attributes of humility are not always high on their list of qualities. Happy, confident children are sure that everything is possible, convinced that their needs will be put first, and determined to achieve their goals, no matter what. They are unafraid to ask for help and willing to try and to fail and to try again. It is only later in life that they begin to measure themselves against others, worry about their abilities and lose that sense of boundless optimism.

When Jesus uses a child as a living illustration of humility, he is not, I believe, expecting his followers to become shy, weak or powerless. The child he shows to his disciples was presumably content to come forward, perhaps delighted to be the centre of attention. This is a child who trusts Jesus and who feels safe in his presence.

We probably all remember the stern warning that Jesus gave to those who would 'put a stumbling block' before such 'little ones', but we might have missed those few crucial words, 'who believe in me' (v. 6, NRSV). Childlike humility in this context seems to be related to a firm and grounded faith – a faith that allows recognition of the divine presence yet is unafraid to draw near; a faith that is simple, direct and straightforward. Can we too recover that childlike humility, knowing that Jesus is greater than us, but utterly convinced that we are loved?

Jesus, help me to come before you today, knowing that I am a cherished child of God. Welcome me, affirm me and fill me with optimism for the future. Let me not stumble or be a stumbling block to others, but instead always run joyfully into your loving presence.

AMANDA BLOOR

Do as I have done

You call me Teacher and Lord – and you are right, for that is what I am. So if I, your Lord and Teacher, have washed your feet, you also ought to wash one another's feet. For I have set you an example, that you also should do as I have done to you. Very truly, I tell you, servants are not greater than their master, nor are messengers greater than the one who sent them.

In Britain, where cool weather means that we enclose our feet in socks and shoes for most of the year and set strict boundaries on appropriate behaviour, the thought of having our feet washed by another – especially someone we respect and look up to – can seem uncomfortably intimate. In the first-century world of the New Testament, where walking on dusty roads in sandalled feet meant that it was polite to clean off the dirt upon entering a house, foot washing was common, but it was a task carried out by slaves. So when Jesus got up during supper and began to wash the feet of his disciples, they were understandably bewildered. Most of the twelve remained silent, but Peter, as always, said what was on his mind: 'You shouldn't do this, Lord!'

Jesus is not dissuaded, but as he sits down, he gives a clear instruction: 'If I have done this for you, then you should do this for one another.' There is to be nothing that is too menial or too humbling between those who follow Jesus. They are to serve one another with gentle respect, regardless of rank or status.

In today's church, we re-enact this moment at services on Maundy Thursday, at ordinations or upon the renewal of priestly vows. For those who dare to unwrap their feet and present them to another, it is a moment of vulnerability: it might be the first time since childhood that they have been washed by another. And for those who are entrusted with the task, there is a sense of awe. It is a moment of shared humility and it brings us close to Christ.

There are no boundaries between us and Christ. How might we break down the barriers that we erect between ourselves and others?

AMANDA BLOOR

Be worthy of your calling

I... beg you to lead a life worthy of the calling to which you have been called, with all humility and gentleness, with patience, bearing with one another in love, making every effort to maintain the unity of the Spirit in the bond of peace. There is one body and one Spirit, just as you were called to the one hope of your calling, one Lord, one faith, one baptism, one God and Father of all...

When we talk about vocation, we often think about a task, career or way of life specific to a particular person and asked of them by God: callings such as ordained ministry, becoming a monk or a nun, or working with the sick, the young or the lonely. We might consider that all of us, as Christians, are called to do something with and for God and each other, but we usually wonder what it is that God has in store uniquely for each one of us. Yet there are corporate callings too, and this passage from the letter to an early Christian community makes it clear that they are all to live out a vocation together – they are to be a church.

It might have been more apparent in the early days of Christianity than it is today that in order to survive and flourish, it was necessary for believers to band together and support one another. This was no simpler in the first century; tensions and irritations would build up and it would be easy for divisions to quickly damage both individual and community alike. Yet if the Ephesians are to fulfil their vocation and be 'worthy' of God's calling to them, they must learn to 'maintain the unity of the Spirit'. They need to treat each other with gentleness and forbearance based upon humility and love.

We too form one body in Christ and are joined together by the one Spirit. When we realise that through God's grace we are equally called, equally loved and equally equipped, there can be no pride or division. We are bonded together in peace.

Help us, Lord, to be worthy of our common calling to be your church.
Come, fill us with your love.

AMANDA BLOOR

81

Stripped, mocked and abused

**After twisting some thorns into a crown, [the soldiers] put it on [Jesus']
head. They put a reed in his right hand and knelt before him and
mocked him, saying, 'Hail, King of the Jews!' They spat on him, and
took the reed and struck him on the head. After mocking him, they
stripped him of the robe and put his own clothes on him. Then they led
him away to crucify him.**

From humble beginnings to a humiliating end, the life of Jesus moves
from birth in a stable to death on a cross. The story, however familiar,
loses none of its power to shock. The one whose birth was foretold by
prophets and heralded by angels, who went about doing good and was
recognised by adoring crowds as the Messiah, is to be executed as a crimi-
nal, a blasphemer, a revolutionary. Betrayed by one of his own and abandoned by his close friends, Jesus is alone and vulnerable. Soldiers gather
around him in force. They mock his kingship by dressing him in a borrowed robe, taunt him with fake subservience, spit at him and jeer. He is
stripped of everything: respect, followers, hope; even the borrowed robe
is torn off. Yet in the midst of this violence and horror, Jesus retains his
dignity.

The authorities wish to humiliate Jesus in order to lessen his influence.
By making an example of him, they hope that he will be seen as weak and
ineffective. But Jesus has an essential humility that comes from his relationship to God and his acceptance of his – and others' – humanity. One
who is genuinely humble cannot be destroyed by humiliation.

Jesus remains silent in the face of provocation and insult; he refuses to
defend himself against false accusation; and at the end he forgives those
who have brought him to the cross. Instead of the teacher from Galilee, it
is his tormentors who are brought low. As Jesus takes his last breath, the
earth shakes and they are terrified. Three days later, a new story begins.

---

*Jesus shows us a way to live in humility and faith, offering us love and
understanding. May we be humble enough to accept him into our lives.*

AMANDA BLOOR

Exploring war and peace

One of the most memorable services I ever took was when I worked as a civilian chaplain to an army regiment in the south of England. As part of my duties I had accompanied a group of young soldiers on a tour of the battlefields of northern France. On the last day of our trip, I led a service of remembrance at Tyne Cot Cemetery, in front of the memorial which stands over lines of white crosses stretching as far as the eye can see. The memorial itself, majestic and solemn, bears the names of 35,000 officers and soldiers whose lives were lost in Belgium between 1914 and 1917, and whose remains could not be found. That's 35,000 sons, husbands and lovers whose loved ones were never able to visit a grave because the scale of the fighting was so great and its nature so horrific that their bodies could not be recovered. That's a very hard fact. Later, I asked one of the soldiers what they had thought of the tour and he replied, 'Well, it's all graveyards, isn't it?' And to some extent he was right. It is very difficult when touring the battlefields of the Somme to rise above the grim weight of statistics – those killed, those injured, the amount of land gained for each life lost. When you add to this the numbers of those killed or wounded in World War II and in subsequent wars, it becomes almost over-powering. Every year since 1939, young men and women, with their whole futures before them, have died in service of their country.

On this centenary of the end of the 'war to end all wars', we find our-selves looking back in sorrow to the carnage of past conflicts, even while we are contemplating new dangers – new types of hidden warfare, such as terrorism – as well as the traditional ones we are all too aware of and fear so much. In the following two weeks, we will look to the Bible to help us understand how we can draw meaning from this and what lessons we can learn while we work for the 'peaceable kingdom', which is God's.

SALLY WELCH

Miserable slaughter

When Herod saw that he had been tricked by the wise men, he was infuriated, and he sent and killed all the children in and around Bethlehem who were two years old or under, according to the time that he had learned from the wise men. Then was fulfilled what had been spoken through the prophet Jeremiah: 'A voice was heard in Ramah, wailing and loud lamentation, Rachel weeping for her children; she refused to be consoled, because they are no more.'

At the end of August 2017 I went to France with my two youngest children, touring the museums and battlefields of World War I. One particularly poignant memorial is a large statue of a dragon, standing at the top of a hill, looking across only about half a mile to Mametz Wood. It marks the spot where the 38th (Welsh) division set off to take Mametz Wood on 7 July 1916 and suffered heavy losses. The wood was cleared of enemies by 14 July but at a cost of over 4,000 casualties. Even 100 years on, to stand where so many people fought and suffered is a very powerful experience. We stood where thousands of people had died just to gain a few hundred yards of land; we stood on green grass where once there had been thick mud, and we wondered at the immensity of the sacrifice that was made.

The story of Herod's vicious slaughter of babies and young children is brutal and shocking. This short, stark chapter in the life of Christ, coming so soon after choirs of angels and rejoicing, is a bleak reminder that Jesus came into a world of brokenness and sin. Yet the very fact of his birth is the sign of hope which had been sought for all the ages – a breaking-in of light and love to the darkness of evil and despair.

As we stand with the peoples of many nations today and remember the end of a fearful conflict that threatened to engulf the world, we lament with Rachel at the loss of life and ponder with Mary the arrival of the light.

'At the going down of the sun and in the morning we will remember them'
('For the Fallen', Robert Laurence Binyon, 1914).

SALLY WELCH

The challenge of remembering

I will call to mind the deeds of the Lord; I will remember your wonders of old. I will meditate on all your work, and muse on your mighty deeds.

Remembering is not always easy. It is not always something we want to do. Those who have never known combat may not want to make the effort to imagine what it may have been like, or to be grateful to those who did engage in it. Those who have lived through war may not want to be reminded of that experience. As a priest, I have had the privilege of listening to people's memories of their own lives and those of their loved ones. During this time I have heard quite a few anecdotes of wartime. People have talked about the different officers they knew and what they thought of them, or about the food that they had to eat and how it was different from that of the Americans. Many, however, found it hard to talk about the details of what actually happened, the real costs: how their comrades died; how their parents, brothers, sisters and friends paid the price of war; and how their own minds and hearts were affected and never again quite the same.

But remembering is important. If we erase the past from our minds, both its successes and its failures, we have no hope of learning from it and, by so doing, building a better future. Psalm 77 explores the use of memory not only as a way of yearning for that which is past and will not return, but also as a source of hope, in that the remembrance of former happiness and contentment can lead to prayers that such times will occur once more. As Christians we can find comfort for the dark times, as we remember instances of God's help in the past, and reassurance in the goodness of his purposes for us. We also find the will to work in partnership with God for a future where warfare is no longer necessary, and peace triumphs over all.

Thank God for times of joy and laughter, which bring us hope and comfort when times are hard.

SALLY WELCH

Honouring the dead

An account of the genealogy of Jesus the Messiah, the son of David, the son of Abraham. Abraham was the father of Isaac, and Isaac the father of Jacob, and Jacob the father of Judah and his brothers, and Judah the father of Perez and Zerah by Tamar, and Perez the father of Hezron, and Hezron the father of Aram, and Aram the father of Aminadab, and Aminadab the father of Nahshon, and Nahshon the father of Salmon, and Salmon the father of Boaz by Rahab, and Boaz the father of Obed by Ruth, and Obed the father of Jesse, and Jesse the father of King David.

Matthew's story of the salvation of the world begins with the recitation of the names of all those people who made such salvation possible – the ancestors of Christ. With the birth of Jesus, the messianic promise of the one who will redeem the fall is fulfilled – the one the world has been waiting for, the one standing on the shoulders of the generations to rescue us from the sin of Adam and restore God's original plan for his creation.

The Canadian National Vimy Memorial is dedicated to the memory of Canadian Expeditionary Force members killed during World War I. It also serves as the place of commemoration for Canadian soldiers killed, or presumed dead, during that war who have no known grave. In all, 11,169 men are remembered. Jane Urquhart's novel *The Stone Carvers* tells of the building of this memorial and relates the poignancy of its construction as the names of the dead are carved into it, names which correspond to 'a cherished, remembered sound called over fields at summer dusk from a back porch door, shouted perhaps in anger or whispered in passion, or in prayer, in the winter dark. All that remained of torn faces, crushed bone, scattered limbs.'

In naming the forebears of Christ, Matthew gives context and meaning to all that has gone before. So too in calling out the names of those who died to bring peace do we honour their efforts and promise to build a better future.

Find your local war memorial and pray for the families whose names are represented on it. 'They shall not grow old, as we that are left grow old' ('For the Fallen', Robert Laurence Binyon, 1914).

SALLY WELCH

A terrible price

But I, O Lord, cry out to you; in the morning my prayer comes before you. O Lord, why do you cast me off? Why do you hide your face from me? Wretched and close to death from my youth up, I suffer your terrors; I am desperate. Your wrath has swept over me; your dread assaults destroy me. They surround me like a flood all day long; from all sides they close in on me. You have caused friend and neighbour to shun me; my companions are in darkness.

In this anniversary year, we have been reminded again of the horrors, the cruelty, the sheer waste of lives expended to gain a few yards of muddy, blood-soaked land. The true cost of war has been made plain to us again and again. And yet we are still paying this price!

The son of a friend of mine is a Royal Navy Marine, and terribly proud of himself. He has learned to drive everything with wheels, from a motorbike to a tank. He can jump out of aeroplanes and dive underwater. But the Navy is also teaching him Arabic, with its possibilities of postings to potentially unstable countries. He has bought his mother a T-shirt that reads: 'You think Marines are tough? Try being the mother of a Marine.'

The words of the psalmist help us to be aware of the cost of war, its horrors, and the fact that the consequences do not end with the end of hostilities but continue to cast a shadow in the lives of thousands of men and women. War is not to be entered into lightly or carelessly, but the battle is still being fought against terrorism, against injustice, and against the bullies, great and small, who try to force others to obey their will, however cruel that will might be. Even in a situation where conflict is inevitable, where in order to preserve the greater good we must fight for it, we must continue to work for peace.

Heavenly Father, help us to work for good in whatever situation
we find ourselves, trusting in Christ's promise to do the same.

SALLY WELCH

The impact of war

O that my head were a spring of water, and my eyes a fountain of tears, so that I might weep day and night for the slain of my poor people!… Take up weeping and wailing for the mountains, and a lamentation for the pastures of the wilderness, beause they are laid waste so that no one passes through, and the lowing of cattle is not heard; both the birds of the air and the animals have fled and are gone.

Some time ago, I visited Arromanches, site of the D-Day landings in 1944, and stood with a group of Royal Engineers on a cliff looking out over the Mulberry harbour, a triumph of wartime engineering. The soldiers had just seen a film of the landings, with all their accompanying chaos and horror, and the two-minute silence held afterwards was in sharp contrast to this. We looked out beyond the memorial to the calm sea, and nothing could be heard except for the skylarks above our heads.

What made the event so poignant was that these soldiers were themselves preparing to go to a conflict zone. This time the country was Afghanistan, but the same possible fate awaited them. My own youngest son was ten days old at the time, and I saw in front of me more young men, sons of mothers just like me. It was an unutterably moving moment, one that brought clearly to life the huge tragedy of war, and its immeasurable impact on those whose lives are drawn into its grip.

Jeremiah the prophet is working overtime to warn his people of the terrible dangers that they face in their faithlessness. The destruction of Jerusalem is prophesied, and his grief is for the punishment the children of Israel will suffer. The effects of war are described in painful detail so that all might take note.

It is easy to view armed conflict as a 'necessary evil', and in doing so to neglect or forget the pain and suffering that are its inevitable consequence. Our role as modern prophets, reminding others of the cost and impact of war, is one which should be taken seriously and practised conscientiously, for the sake of all people.

Lord, make me a peacemaker.

SALLY WELCH

Looking for a different way (part 1)

'This is my commandment, that you love one another as I have loved you. No one has greater love than this, to lay down one's life for one's friends… You did not choose me but I chose you. And I appointed you to go and bear fruit, fruit that will last, so that the Father will give you whatever you ask him in my name. I am giving you these commands so that you may love one another.'

Of course, the disciples did not know then how much Jesus loved them. They did not know how he would suffer and die for them, nor that the love he commanded them to bear for one another would be one that demanded such great personal sacrifice. We are not promised that living a Christian life will be easy; we are not promised that we will be spared the experience of suffering or evil. We are promised only that we have been chosen by Christ, and 'appointed… to go and bear fruit'. We must bear the fruit of a great, sacrificial love, not only for those we know but for those we will never know; not only for the worthy but for the unworthy, in the name of Christ.

The 2016 film *Hacksaw Ridge* tells the story of Desmond Doss, a conscientious objector who, during the Battle of Okinawa, rescued 75 men, lowering them by a single rope from an enemy-occupied ridge to safety. Doss found a way to live according to his beliefs which still offered him the opportunity to serve his country and help his fellow soldiers – a way which offers an example even today.

We may not have a loud voice in the public arena, but we can pray for a different way from that of warfare as a solution to a problem, and live out that prayer by seeking peaceful resolutions to conflict, whether in our private lives, in our workplace or in whatever public sphere we operate. One individual makes a small difference – many small differences will change the world.

'Please, Lord, let me get one more' (words uttered by Private Doss each time another soldier is rescued).

SALLY WELCH

Looking for a different way (part 2)

'Thus he has shown the mercy promised to our ancestors, and has remembered his holy covenant, the oath that he swore to our ancestor Abraham, to grant us that we, being rescued from the hands of our enemies, might serve him without fear, in holiness and righteousness before him all our days.'

As we read Zechariah's joyful hymn as he looks forward to the coming of the Messiah, we witness the juxtaposition of the old covenant and the new, the promise and the fulfilment. We can be consoled not only by the reflection that one generation is always succeeded by another with new ideas and visions, but by the hope expressed here which transcends death itself. This reminds us that however dark the times we may be living in, emotionally, physically or spiritually, the light of hope and love cannot be extinguished.

As we journey further in our exploration of war and peace, we encounter again a different way, one which moves away from anger and conflict and embraces harmony and tolerance. This way is open to us all, through the grace of God. We need simply to ask.

The Battle of Goose Green took place in May 1982 during the Falklands War. The soldiers of the Second Parachute Regiment were pinned down, outnumbered three to one, and had been awake for more than 40 hours. They were running out of ammunition when the commanding officer was hit. Colonel Keeble took command, but before he issued any orders, he walked a little way off and prayed, 'My Father, I abandon myself to you. Do with me as you will. Whatever you may do with me, I thank you, provided your will is fulfilled. I ask for nothing more.' Then he returned to his command post and told two POWs that they were to return to their lines and tell their commanders that, as they were going to lose this war, the best thing to do would be to surrender. After negotiation of a surrender that left the Argentinians with some dignity and an opportunity to mourn their dead, the battle was finished and the imprisoned British civilians freed.

'Blessed are the peacemakers' (Matthew 5:9).

SALLY WELCH

Living by the Spirit

By contrast, the fruit of the Spirit is love, joy, peace, patience, kindness, generosity, faithfulness, gentleness, and self-control. There is no law against such things… If we live by the Spirit, let us also be guided by the Spirit.

I was speaking recently to a man whose wife was in a nursing home, suffering from dementia. Every day he visited her, sitting by her bed, reading to her, calming her when she was angry and abusive, comforting her when she was distressed and confused. I told him how brave I thought he was, which he vehemently denied. 'I'm only doing my duty,' he replied. 'When we married I swore I would look after her, and I will.'

Stories of two world wars abound just now as people reflect on the way the world was changed by these huge conflicts. We hear of bravery and self-sacrifice, and we learn of instances of cruelty and cowardice. Of such are battles – and life – composed. Stories of ordinary people who in extraordinary times perform deeds beyond imagining can light up not just their period of history but our current times. But there remain hundreds of thousands of stories untold – those which feature nothing outstanding but a determination by ordinary people to do their duty, which yet form the bedrock of daily life, upon which others can lean and find support.

As we listen and respond to tales of ingenuity and derring-do, let us draw inspiration from the actions of others and determine to live bravely within our own circumstances. May we who have been given the gift of the Spirit live out that gift in our daily lives, exercising love and patience when perhaps we are running low on both, behaving gently and generously when our inclination is to do neither. Then our lives too will become examples from which others can draw strength and find hope.

'Oh, master, grant that I may never seek so much to be consoled as to console, to be understood as to understand, to be loved as to love with all my soul' (from a prayer by St Francis).

SALLY WELCH

War and peace in everyday life

When Jesus saw the crowds, he went up the mountain; and after he sat down, his disciples came to him. Then he began to speak, and taught them, saying: 'Blessed are the poor in spirit, for theirs is the kingdom of heaven. Blessed are those who mourn, for they will be comforted. Blessed are the meek, for they will inherit the earth. Blessed are those who hunger and thirst for righteousness, for they will be filled. Blessed are the merciful, for they will receive mercy. Blessed are the pure in heart, for they will see God. Blessed are the peacemakers, for they will be called children of God. Blessed are those who are persecuted for righteousness' sake, for theirs is the kingdom of heaven.'

Our local church is open during the day, and visitors are invited to write in a book what effect the place has had upon them. The most common adjective used is 'peaceful'. When I commented on this, one stalwart of the congregation replied wryly, 'They should try being here on a Sunday!'

People who seek peace by joining a church are often shocked by the turbulence of emotions and occasional resentments they find within such a community. This isn't really surprising – it's often a byproduct of the fact that churches are one of the few places where different people of different backgrounds are brought together. As with families at Christmas it would be surprising if there weren't a row or two! Living in community isn't easy; being a peacemaker often brings about those feelings which are far from peaceful – anger, hurt or exhaustion. Careful negotiations must be entered into, compromises need to be made, old wounds should be forgiven, insults must be forgotten. However, peace-making is a vocation to which all Christians are called, a challenge thrown out to us by the Son of God as he stood before the crowd that day so long ago and gave us a matrix for life, a scaffold around which to build our everyday thoughts and actions, raising a structure of love to act as an example of hope and light to those around us.

'Peace I leave with you; my peace I give to you' (John 14:27, NRSV).

SALLY WELCH

Forgive me

One of the criminals who were hanged there kept deriding [Jesus] and saying, 'Are you not the Messiah? Save yourself and us!' But the other rebuked him, saying, 'Do you not fear God, since you are under the same sentence of condemnation? And we indeed have been condemned justly, for we are getting what we deserve for our deeds, but this man has done nothing wrong.' Then he said, 'Jesus, remember me when you come into your kingdom.' He replied, 'Truly I tell you, today you will be with me in Paradise.'

This single moment in history, when a sinner begs forgiveness and is promised paradise, is perhaps one of the most moving moments there is, and one which offers such hope to us all!

One of the most common reasons I hear from people for not going to church is that they are not good enough, to which I respond that I go to church for that same reason! Nonetheless, forgiving themselves for past errors remains a challenge for many people. A former soldier, who had landed in Sicily towards the end of 1944 and fought his way up through Italy to Rome, reported sadly to me that he still had nightmares about the things he had done during that time. A kind, gentle man, he was tolerant of others partly because he was so aware of his own shortcomings, but his lack of self-forgiveness meant he felt unable to take part in church community life, to the deprivation of both himself and the congregation he remained outside of. It was only after much prayer that he was able to accept God's forgiveness, offered freely to him, as it is held out to all by Christ as he hangs on the cross, suffering on our behalf in order to free us from our foolishness and sin.

When we have the courage to accept our redemption, then we become truly able to fulfil our potential as God's children, reaching out in love to those who still live in darkness and leading them into the light.

'To be a Christian means to forgive the inexcusable because God has forgiven the inexcusable in you' (C.S. Lewis, The Weight of Glory*).*

SALLY WELCH

How many times?

'Be on your guard! If another disciple sins, you must rebuke the offender, and if there is repentance, you must forgive. And if the same person sins against you seven times a day, and turns back to you seven times and says, "I repent," you must forgive.' The apostles said to the Lord, 'Increase our faith!'

Those poor disciples! How hard it is to forgive, even once, when someone has sinned against you! But once is not enough. Even if they are sinned against seven times in one day, each time those words 'I repent' are uttered, then the disciples 'must forgive'. No wonder they beg Jesus, 'Increase our faith'!

Forgiveness is not easy. In fact, it's hardly possible for us in our natural state, when it's so much easier simply to nurse the grudge, feed the resentment and cherish the ill feeling. But that way leads only to bitterness and conflict, damaging both the sinner and the one who is sinned against. It is only when we turn our perceptions on their heads, when we remember how much God has given us, how his mercy and grace have filled our lives, that we will be able to put aside our wrath and our hurt and move on in wholeness.

We may not be able to pray the following prayer ourselves, so full as it is with love and compassion. We may still be too raw; the hurts may be too deep for us to offer forgiveness to those who have offended us. Yet we can stand at the foot of the cross and ask God to forgive on our behalf: 'Father, forgive them; for they do not know what they are doing' (Luke 23:34, NRSV).

'Lord, remember not only the men and women of good will, but also those of ill will. But do not only remember the suffering they have inflicted on us. Remember the fruits we have brought, thanks to this suffering – our comradeship, our loyalty, our humility; the courage, the generosity, the greatness of heart which have grown out of all this. And when they come to judgement, let all the fruits we have borne be their forgiveness' (reportedly found in Ravensbrück death camp near the body of a child).

SALLY WELCH

Remember – then decide

[Joshua] said, 'Then put away the foreign gods that are among you, and incline your hearts to the Lord, the God of Israel.' The people said to Joshua, 'The Lord our God we will serve, and him we will obey.' So Joshua made a covenant with the people that day, and made statutes and ordinances for them at Shechem.

Joshua has reminded the Israelites how God treated them: how he chose Abraham, Isaac and Jacob; how he cared for the imprisoned Joseph and noticed the suffering of the people in Egypt; how he fed them in the wilderness and brought them into the promised land. He remembers all this, then calls the people to choose whether to be true to the God who has shown them such mercy or to worship the idols with which they are surrounded.

Today we remember – and we are called to make much the same choice Joshua called the people of Israel to make. We are called to choose life or death – to decide for God and the things of God or for ourselves and the things of the world. We are called to work for justice and righteousness, to take the narrow way of truth-seeking and avoid the broad way of easy compromise and neglect. We can stand alongside the suffering and the vulnerable or turn our heads away as we walk past, leaving them stranded on the roadside.

Together with all God's people we are called to remember how God has treated us in the past, and to respond with a commitment to the future. We remember the sacrifices others have made in the name of peace, and ask for the grace to resist evil within ourselves and our communities, giving ourselves completely for the sake of God's kingdom.

---

*'Peace is the beauty of life. It is sunshine. It is the smile of a child,
the love of a mother, the joy of a father, the togetherness of a family.
It is the advancement of man, the victory of a just cause, the triumph
of truth. Peace is all of these and more and more'
(Menachem Begin, Nobel Peace Prize Lecture 1978).*

SALLY WELCH

'I believe in the sun'

And war broke out in heaven; Michael and his angels fought against the dragon. The dragon and his angels fought back, but they were defeated, and there was no longer any place for them in heaven. The great dragon was thrown down, that ancient serpent, who is called the Devil and Satan, the deceiver of the whole world – he was thrown down to the earth, and his angels were thrown down with him.

What a wonderful message! Wrapped as it is in the poetic imagery of dragons and ancient serpents, devils and angels, we may be tempted to disregard this piece of scripture along with those other parts of the Bible that we find difficult or challenging. But it carries within it all that we need to sustain hope in dark times. For God is still God and will remain God for ever.

The all-decisive battle in heaven between good and evil has already been fought, and the outcome is assured. Evil will not triumph – it never has and it never will – because the victory of good reaches beyond time and enfolds eternity. There is rejoicing in heaven, and we echo that rejoicing because we are citizens of heaven and a place is assured for us there.

There may be grievous troubles on earth, but these are the death throes of the defeated one, the final lashing out in anger and despair of the beaten. We may be assailed and at times feel overwhelmed by the consequences of our sin and the sins of others, the consequence of living between the 'now' and the 'not yet' of the kingdom, but we will not be overcome.

We must hold in our hearts the ideal of the kingdom, an ideal to aim for and work towards – that vision of God's will being done 'on earth as it is in heaven' (Matthew 6:10, NRSV) – believing that every little counts: every loving word, every prayer, every tiny baby born in a manger, destined to save the world.

'I believe in the sun, even when it is not shining
And I believe in love, even when there's no one there.
And I believe in God, even when he is silent'
(Anonymous, World War II).

SALLY WELCH

Shalom

Then I saw a new heaven and a new earth; for the first heaven and the first earth had passed away, and the sea was no more. And I saw the holy city, the new Jerusalem, coming down out of heaven from God, prepared as a bride adorned for her husband. And I heard a loud voice from the throne saying, 'See, the home of God is among mortals. He will dwell with them; they will be his peoples, and God himself will be with them; he will wipe every tear from their eyes. Death will be no more; mourning and crying and pain will be no more, for the first things have passed away.'

The book of Revelation is richly strange and wonderful, originally written to encourage those who were suffering acutely for their faith. The writer assures us that the suffering of this world is temporary, and it will be ended when God's judgement comes on earth. Then, when that has been effected, we come to the words of Revelation 21: 'Then I saw a new heaven and a new earth.' These words are an inspiration, a goal for us to work towards. The new earth will be a place where justice and freedom have sovereignty, where the old ways have ceased and where we will live in peace with each other and with God.

At the moment we only experience an echo of this peace, occasional glimpses of the extraordinary gift of *shalom* that is offered to us through the life, death and resurrection of Christ. *Shalom* is the act of living in harmony with God, with creation, with each other and with ourselves. In our current damaged, sinful world it is only a promise, but it is a promise which Christians are heir to and must commit to working for.

Living peacefully together, living with other people, always holds challenges, but while the will exists to create something worthwhile and significant, these difficulties can be overcome – all that is needed is to cultivate an attitude of tolerance and forgiveness, and a vision for the future: 'The ultimate test of a moral society is the kind of world that it leaves to its children' (Dietrich Bonhoeffer).

'When you go home tell them of us and say,
for your tomorrow we gave our today' (Kohima Epitaph).

SALLY WELCH

Leviticus

Leviticus is rarely quoted in the New Testament, except 19:18 ('Love your neighbour as yourself,' Mark 12:31, NIV), but its world view and the sacrificial system it describes are integral to understanding the person and work of Jesus. For this reason it is worth exploring what it has to offer. We get our modern title from the Latin *Liber Leviticus*, the Book of the Levites, which draws on a rabbinical tradition that the book was for the instruction of the priests (who are members of the tribe of Levi). It is part of a larger body of work beginning in Exodus and continuing into Numbers. However, most of the book is not addressed to priests, but to the people of Israel as a whole: 'when any of you brings an animal...'

Leviticus is set during the period when the Israelites are in the wilderness, between Egypt and the promised land, and the events that happened on Mount Sinai are key. Recent scholarship has been indebted to the writing of the anthropologist Mary Douglas (*Leviticus as Literature*, Oxford University Press, 1999), who suggests that understanding Leviticus rests on understanding relational meanings, such as between Sinai, the tent of meeting and the temple. The first week explores the background to the world of Leviticus.

While the world view that Leviticus puts forward was shared with many other peoples of the ancient Near East, it also differed radically in key aspects. Most communities had many different gods, but Leviticus has only one; many religions suggested the idea of demons to explain why things failed, but Leviticus suggests that 'impurity' was the root cause of failure and that there are no other authorities beyond God. The book is essentially about how God relates to his covenant people and how they are expected to live in response.

The importance of the book for Christians is to understand how this world view changed with the coming of Christ. The strict separation between the divine and the ordinary, represented by the curtain separating the holy of holies from the rest of the sanctuary, was rent in two at the crucifixion (Mark 15:38), symbolising the beginning of God's new relationship with his people. The second week explores how Leviticus influences Christian theology and contemporary issues.

NICK READ

Relational meaning

The Lord said to Moses, 'I am going to come to you in a dense cloud, so that the people will hear me speaking with you and will always put their trust in you.'… 'Put limits for the people around the mountain and tell them, "Be careful that you do not approach the mountain or touch the foot of it. Whoever touches the mountain is to be put to death."… Only when the ram's horn sounds a long blast may they approach the mountain.'… The Lord descended to the top of Mount Sinai and called Moses to the top of the mountain. So Moses went up and the Lord said to him, 'Go down and warn the people so they do not force their way through to see the Lord and many of them perish. Even the priests, who approach the Lord, must consecrate themselves, or the Lord will break out against them.'

Key to Leviticus are the events on Mount Sinai, when God ratified the covenant and gave the law. There were strict limitations imposed on where the people, the priests and Moses were permitted to go. What lies behind this is an understanding that the divine and the ordinary were not permitted to mix but needed to remain separate. The 'pattern' of Sinai is repeated in the design of the tent of meeting (the mobile temple in the wilderness) and that of the temple built in Jerusalem, with an outer court, where all people could gather (like the foot of the mountain); the sanctuary reserved for priests (similar to the lower slopes of Sinai); and the holy of holies, which only the high priest could enter once a year (echoing the summit, where only Moses was permitted).

This pattern seems strange at first, but we continue to use it in many places of worship today, dividing the sanctuary (which means 'sacred place') from the nave, or creating specific places for prayer and reflection. The challenge for many of us is to create such spaces within the busyness and fullness of our daily lives.

Lord, help me to create space today for prayer,
reflection and the development of holiness.

NICK READ

Sacrifice and value

You are to lay your hand on the head of your offering and slaughter it at the entrance to the tent of meeting. Then Aaron's sons the priests shall splash the blood against the sides of the altar. From the fellowship offering you are to bring a food offering to the Lord: the internal organs and all the fat that is connected to them, both kidneys with the fat on them near the loins, and the long lobe of the liver, which you will remove with the kidneys. Then Aaron's sons are to burn it on the altar on top of the burnt offering that is lying on the burning wood; it is a food offering, an aroma pleasing to the Lord.

Deuteronomy distinguishes between sacrifices and killing for food (Deuteronomy 12:15). Leviticus, however, stresses that whenever an animal's blood is shed, its life must be valued as an act of sacrifice. The book appears quite daunting, containing chapters of instruction about which parts of the animals may be used and how they are to be arranged on the altar. What lies behind this is an understanding that all life belongs to God alone, and that no life (not even that of an animal) should be taken without due reverence. The detailed instructions are directed at those who raise and slaughter the animal and are designed to ensure that respect and honour are properly given.

Mary Douglas, an anthropologist who wrote about Leviticus, suggests that the dismembering of the animal conforms to relational meaning. Blood was where the life force resided and therefore belongs exclusively to God. 'I will set my face against any Israelite or any foreigner residing among them who eats blood, and I will cut them off from the people. For the life of a creature is in the blood…' (Leviticus 17:10–11, NIV). Blood, and key organs such as the kidneys, are therefore analogous to the holy places and must be handled by priests (who deal with the holy), while the peripheral parts of the animal are available for anyone to consume.

Lord, in this age of fast food remind me of the value of all life.

NICK READ

Holiness (part 1)

The sin offering is to be slaughtered before the Lord in the place where the burnt offering is slaughtered; it is most holy. The priest who offers it shall eat it; it is to be eaten in the sanctuary area, in the courtyard of the tent of meeting. Whatever touches any of the flesh will become holy, and if any of the blood is spattered on a garment, you must wash it in the sanctuary area.

In the world of Leviticus, the holy and the ordinary must remain separate. The priests are empowered to deal with the holy but only under strict circumstances, which are codified in chapters 6 and 7. Holiness was a transferable quality, in that whoever touched holy things would assimilate its characteristics, but it was not to be sought lightly or dealt with in a cavalier fashion. It required designated people (priests), designated places (the tent of meeting) and designated ritual (the burnt offering) to contain its effects.

What lies behind this is an understanding of God's awesome majesty and power, which transcends anything that we might experience and be able to cope with, and which is not something to trifle with. When the law was given on Mount Sinai, Moses was warned that if the people forced their way on to the mountain they would perish and that 'even the priests, who approach the Lord, must consecrate themselves, or the Lord will break out against them' (Exodus 19:21–22, NIV).

It is a measure of God's love for his people that he created the conditions by which this gulf was closed, and that, while the transcendence of God remains, we are all empowered to know him intimately through the love of Christ. The holiness of God remains absolute, but we have been enabled to share in that divine attribute as adopted sons and daughters.

Let us give thanks, because 'God's dwelling-place is now among the people, and he will dwell with them. They will be his people, and God himself will be with them and be their God. "He will wipe every tear from their eyes"' (Revelation 21:3–4, NIV).

NICK READ

Holiness (part 2)

The Lord said to Moses, 'Speak to the entire assembly of Israel and say to them: "Be holy because I, the Lord your God, am holy. Each of you must respect your mother and father, and you must observe my Sabbaths. I am the Lord your God. Do not turn to idols or make metal gods for yourselves. I am the Lord your God. When you sacrifice a fellowship offering to the Lord, sacrifice it in such a way that it will be accepted on your behalf. It shall be eaten on the day you sacrifice it or on the next day; anything left over until the third day must be burned. If any of it is eaten on the third day, it is impure and will not be accepted.'

The later chapters of Leviticus contain a textual work known as the holiness code. Holiness is an attribute of God, and all holiness ultimately derives from God. Therefore, if the people are to live with God they need to be holy as well. Holiness embodies two ideas: something pure and clean and something which is separated from the ordinary. To be holy is to be set apart for God.

Separation is not negative, but constitutes a new and distinctive relationship. The Hebrew term for holiness, *kadusha*, is invoked by the making of *Kiddush*, the sanctifying blessing offered over a cup of wine at the beginning of the Sabbath, and in *Kiddushin*, the betrothal between a couple to be married. In both cases the emphasis is on what is being created – the Sabbath day, the marriage – rather than on what is left behind. Separation takes place to ensure a closer relationship with God. It also has a sense of immediacy – a fellowship offering to the Lord is effective for only two days, and by the third day it is no longer valid. Cultivating holiness is to be a daily requirement for God's people not a future aspiration.

Jesus rephrases Leviticus 19:2 as 'Be perfect… as your heavenly Father is perfect' (Matthew 5:48, NIV) and makes himself the focus, inviting us to 'Come to me' (Matthew 11:28, NIV) and 'Follow me' (Matthew 4:19, NIV).

What should I leave and what should I embrace today?

NICK READ

Clean and unclean

'"I will give [the land] to you as an inheritance, a land flowing with milk and honey." I am the Lord your God, who has set you apart from the nations. You must therefore make a distinction between clean and unclean animals and between unclean and clean birds. Do not defile yourselves by any animal or bird or anything that moves along the ground – those that I have set apart as unclean for you. You are to be holy to me because I, the Lord, am holy, and I have set you apart from the nations to be my own.'

In the NIV translation of Leviticus 11, all of life (from land, water and air) is divided into clean and unclean. Cleanness is a category not a condition. Priests who become unclean are barred from the holy places until they have been cleansed. It applies to childbirth and menstruation, skin diseases and bodily discharges (chapters 12—15).

The categorisation of animals that are clean appears quite arbitrary (e.g. animals with split hooves that chew the cud), but this may simply reflect an exercise in God's sovereign will since it is God who decides what is clean and unclean. Being unclean does not mean separation from God's care, since in Genesis 6 unclean animals are still brought into the ark and every living creature is included within the covenant (Genesis 9:12), but being clean is a prerequisite for approaching the holy. Therefore, only clean animals can be offered as sacrifices (i.e. set apart for God), and only clean animals can be eaten (i.e. set apart for us) if the people are to be holy as God is holy. The world of Leviticus is comprehensive and every aspect of life is to be governed by the demands of the covenant relationship with God.

Peter's vision in Acts 10:10–16, in which all animals are declared to be clean, does not repudiate the understanding of Leviticus but demonstrates the comprehensiveness of God's salvation through Christ. Because of the cross, all of creation has been set apart for God, so all of creation is able to approach the holy.

Thank God for the breadth of earth's salvation.

NICK READ

Atonement

'Aaron is to offer the bull for his own sin offering to make atonement for himself and his household. Then he is to take the two goats and present them before the Lord at the entrance to the tent of meeting. He is to cast lots for the two goats – one lot for the Lord and the other for the scapegoat. Aaron shall bring the goat whose lot falls to the Lord and sacrifice it for a sin offering. But the goat chosen by lot as the scapegoat shall be presented alive before the Lord to be used for making atonement by sending it into the wilderness as a scapegoat.'

Azazel, 'the scapegoat', is part of God's instructions regarding the Day of Atonement, in which the high priest offers a sacrifice for himself, his household and the sins of the nation. Two goats are chosen by lot and the first goat is sacrificed and its blood used to cleanse the most holy place, the tent of meeting and the altar (Leviticus 16:20). The other, live, goat is brought to the priest, who lays hands upon it and confesses all of the wickedness and rebellion of the people before it is sent into the wilderness, in the charge of someone appointed for the task, so that 'the goat will carry on itself all their sins to a remote place' (Leviticus 16:22, NIV).

Both goats together articulate the nature of atonement, of being made right with God. One goat is a sacrifice, where the shedding of blood acknowledges the cost of sin for which propitiation or appeasement is required to meet the demands of justice and righteousness. The other goat has the people's sins symbolically placed upon it and is released into the desert, embodying the idea that the power and reality of sin are removed from the sinner – 'as far as the east is from the west' (Psalm 103:12, NIV). While the sacrifice of the first goat takes place in private, with only the high priest being present, the release of the second goat is a public proclamation.

Thank the Lord for the inner cleansing and outward joy of our atonement.

NICK READ

The burnt offering

'If the offering is a burnt offering from the flock, from either the sheep or the goats, you are to offer a male without defect. You are to slaughter it at the north side of the altar before the Lord, and Aaron's sons the priests shall splash its blood against the sides of the altar. You are to cut it into pieces, and the priest shall arrange them, including the head and the fat, on the wood that is burning on the altar. You are to wash the internal organs and the legs with water, and the priest is to bring all of them and burn them on the altar. It is a burnt offering, a food offering, an aroma pleasing to the Lord.'

Noah sacrificed a burnt offering after the flood (Genesis 8:20–22), and Abraham was commanded to present his son Isaac as a burnt offering, though God substituted a ram (Genesis 22). Burnt offerings were numerous, scheduled each morning and evening (Exodus 29:38–42), on various feast days and on the Sabbath. They were often in conjunction with other sacrifices such as guilt or sin offerings. People identified with the animal by placing hands on its head before it was slaughtered, and the sacrifice was to cleanse those ritually impure, reflecting humanity's alienation from God.

The Hebrew *korban*, sometimes translated 'holocaust', means to ascend in smoke. It contains two ideas: that the animal was completely transformed by the process of burning (only the hide was retained), and that it became 'an aroma pleasing to the Lord'. Micah 6.6–8 reminds the people that this is meant to represent their faithfulness to God in acting justly, loving mercy and walking humbly, and the apostle Paul proclaims, 'I may... give up my body to be burned [i.e. sacrificed] – but if I have no love, this does me no good' (1 Corinthians 13:3, GNT). Christian authors use the burnt offering to help explain the significance of Christ's Passion, in which Jesus' physical life was consumed as he ascended to God on behalf of humanity.

'Follow God's example, therefore, as dearly loved children and live a life of love, just as Christ loved us and gave himself up for us as a fragrant offering and sacrifice to God' (Ephesians 5:1–2, NIV).

NICK READ

The grain offering

'Every grain offering you bring to the Lord must be made without yeast, for you are not to burn any yeast or honey in a food offering presented to the Lord. You may bring them to the Lord as an offering of the firstfruits, but they are not to be offered on the altar as a pleasing aroma. Season all your grain offerings with salt. Do not leave the salt of the covenant of your God out of your grain offerings; add salt to all your offerings. If you bring a grain offering of firstfruits to the Lord, offer crushed heads of new grain roasted in the fire. Put oil and incense on it; it is a grain offering.'

The grain offering is usually presented in conjunction with the burnt offering (Numbers 28:4–5). Since no blood is involved its principal purpose is not about sin but about hope and dependence. For this nomadic people, grain and incense are probably more precious and rare than cattle or sheep. Nevertheless, they are to offer the very best fine flour (Leviticus 2:1) and, if it is naturally occurring ('the firstfruits'), to augment it with expensive frankincense. No leaven or honey are to be added, possibly a reference to corruption or contamination and a reminder of the unleavened bread at Passover.

Salt symbolises the covenant, because it preserves and purifies (Numbers 18:19), and the sacrifice reminds them of the covenant promise leading them to a promised land (Deuteronomy 11:10–12). However, that is still in the future, and this costly sacrifice of fine flour and incense is a reminder to trust in God's provision until then. Deuteronomy 26:3–5 recalls how, after they settled in the promised land, they changed the ritual to remind themselves of how God had provided for them in the wilderness.

Christ also asked his followers to trust, asking God to 'give us today our daily bread' (Matthew 6:11, NIV), and the apostle Paul refers to the gift of money from the Philippians in sacrificial terms as 'a fragrant offering, an acceptable sacrifice, pleasing to God' (Philippians 4:18, NIV).

What would be the equivalent of a grain offering for your walk with God, where you need to exercise trust in his continuing care?

NICK READ

The peace offering

'If your offering is a fellowship offering, and you offer an animal from the herd, whether male or female, you are to present before the Lord an animal without defect. You are to lay your hand on the head of your offering and slaughter it at the entrance to the tent of meeting. Then Aaron's sons the priests shall splash the blood against the sides of the altar. From the fellowship offering you are to bring a food offering to the Lord: the internal organs and all the fat that is connected to them, both kidneys with the fat on them near the loins, and the long lobe of the liver, which you will remove with the kidneys. Then Aaron's sons are to burn it on the altar on top of the burnt offering that is lying on the burning wood; it is a food offering, an aroma pleasing to the Lord.'

A fellowship or peace offering is optional, arising from the desire of the person to offer thanksgiving (Leviticus 7:12–15), or because of a vow that has been taken (Leviticus 7:16–17). The parts of the animal offered in the peace offering are always placed on the altar on top of the day's burnt offering and grain offering, symbolising that fellowship is only possible in the first place because of the removal of sin and guilt.

The text in Leviticus deals with the mechanics (chapter 3) and the meaning (chapter 7), together with the respective roles of the worshipper and priest. The offering ends with a meal in which the priest (representing God), the worshipper and his family and friends sit down together to eat. The symbolism is of completeness, where God and people partake together of a satisfying meal. Understandably the offering is aligned to times of joyfulness, such as Solomon's feasts for his servants (1 Kings 3:15) and marriage.

This contributes to our understanding of the Eucharist (the word means thanksgiving), which also stresses that Christ was given for humanity (an offering), resulting in harmonious fellowship with God.

'Peace be with you! As the Father has sent me, I am sending you'
(John 20:21, NIV).

NICK READ

The sin offering

'If the whole Israelite community sins unintentionally and does what is forbidden in any of the Lord's commands, even though the community is unaware of the matter, when they realise their guilt and the sin they committed becomes known, the assembly must bring a young bull as a sin offering and present it before the tent of meeting. The elders of the community are to lay their hands on the bull's head before the Lord, and the bull shall be slaughtered before the Lord. Then the anointed priest is to take some of the bull's blood into the tent of meeting. He shall dip his finger into the blood and sprinkle it before the Lord seven times in front of the curtain. He is to put some of the blood on the horns of the altar that is before the Lord in the tent of meeting. The rest of the blood he shall pour out at the base of the altar of burnt offering at the entrance to the tent of meeting.'

We often think of sin as something that is intentional, but the Bible also thinks of sin as arising through ignorance of God's demands. Even unintentional sin provides a barrier between humanity and God's holiness. In Leviticus 4 the sacrifices under discussion are those offered in response to these 'unwitting' or 'unintentional' sins (Leviticus 4:2). Why should these be of concern to God? Perhaps partly because what is often called ignorance is in fact a reflection of the power of sin, in that the fall of humanity has created conditions in which ignorance of God has become part of 'normal' life. Therefore, if we are to respond to God we need to acknowledge our 'ignorance' and seek help.

Leviticus recognises this and also the role of the community in supporting individuals. The sacrifices vary depending on the persons affected: priests (Leviticus 4:3), the community (Leviticus 4:13), political authorities (Leviticus 4:22) or common people (Leviticus 4:27).

'We have left undone those things which we ought to have done,
and we have done those things which we ought not to have done,
and there is no health in us. But thou, O Lord, have mercy upon us'
(Book of Common Prayer).

NICK READ

The guilt offering

'If anyone sins and is unfaithful to the Lord by deceiving a neighbour about something entrusted to them or left in their care or about something stolen, or if they cheat their neighbour, or if they find lost property and lie about it, or if they swear falsely... they must return what they have stolen or taken by extortion, or what was entrusted to them, or the lost property they found, or whatever it was they swore falsely about. They must make restitution in full, add a fifth of the value to it and give it all to the owner on the day they present their guilt offering. And as a penalty they must bring to the priest, that is, to the Lord, their guilt offering, a ram from the flock, one without defect and of the proper value.'

Jesus said the two greatest commandments were to love the Lord your God and to love your neighbour as yourself (Matthew 22:37–40). Leviticus understands that defrauding a neighbour is also to defraud God, since God's concern extends to all people and 'the foreigner residing among you must be treated as your native-born. Love them as yourself' (Leviticus 19:34, NIV). Therefore, the remedy for these sorts of sins must take both God and neighbour into account, requiring a guilt offering to the Lord and restitution to the person defrauded.

We often think of the Old Testament as legalistic, but the rabbis who commented on these passages asked whether financial restitution was a precondition of God's forgiveness or the result of God's forgiveness. In other words, do we pay someone back in order to be forgiven or is it forgiveness that enables us to make restitution? The story of Jesus' meeting with Zacchaeus the tax collector (Luke 19:1–10) tells of a man whose encounter with God led him to pay back what he owed and more. Forgiveness creates the possibility of new life.

'You were taught, with regard to your former way of life, to put off your old self, which is being corrupted by its deceitful desires; to be made new in the attitude of your minds; and to put on the new self, created to be like God in true righteousness and holiness' (Ephesians 4:22–24, NIV).

NICK READ

Childbirth

The Lord said to Moses, 'Say to the Israelites: "A woman who becomes pregnant and gives birth to a son will be ceremonially unclean for seven days, just as she is unclean during her monthly period. On the eighth day the boy is to be circumcised. Then the woman must wait thirty-three days to be purified from her bleeding. She must not touch anything sacred or go to the sanctuary until the days of her purification are over."'

These are difficult verses that seem to imply that pregnancy and childbirth are bad things, by which someone becomes 'unclean'. However, that is to infer that clean and unclean represent moral qualities, which is not the case. This text occurs within a series of chapters (12—15) that at first sight appear to be entirely unconnected, dealing with reproduction, leprosy and mildew! But the relational meaning is that they all deal with the integrity of things and what happens at the boundaries of the body or the structure.

The Israelites wrote about sex because they understood its importance, and the significance of losing vital fluids, such as at birth and menstruation, is that it is a barrier to fertility, which is part of the covenant blessing. Furthermore, the woman's blood represents the life force (that which remains exclusively God's) and yet in childbirth that force is being transmitted to another. We also tend to focus on the language of 'clean' and 'unclean' and overlook the fact that a woman who is ritually unclean will thereby be enabled to have a period of rest, because her uncleanness limits what she can do.

Far from implying that pregnancy and birth are bad things, Leviticus recognises that the act of giving birth is something that occurs at the boundaries of the holy and the ordinary, when life is transferred from one to another, and that it requires its own designated rituals. There is no contradiction, therefore, that when Jesus was born his circumcision and Mary's purification (Luke 2:21–24) followed the Levitical prescriptions.

Give thanks to the Lord for the wonder of childbirth,
the mystery of life and the blessing of motherhood.

NICK READ

Covenant blessing and ecological health

'I am the Lord. If you follow my decrees and are careful to obey my commands, I will send you rain in its season, and the ground will yield its crops and the trees their fruit. Your threshing will continue until grape harvest and the grape harvest will continue until planting, and you will eat all the food you want and live in safety in your land.'

Leviticus contains important truths about the relationships between God, humanity and the planet. Obedience to the covenant lies behind all facets of human existence and practice, and one of the blessings such obedience confers is ecological health, as human fidelity and the natural world are interwoven within God's providence. Thus faithful obedience brings the blessing of seasonal rains, abundance and safety. Conversely, disobedience to the covenant would bring ecological ill-health. Isaiah, in line with many of the prophets, proclaims: 'The earth dries up and withers, the world languishes and withers, the heavens languish with the earth. The earth is defiled by its people; they have disobeyed the laws, violated the statutes and broken the everlasting covenant' (Isaiah 24:4–5, NIV).

The church's theological response to climate change also asserts that we face this unparalleled crisis because we have ignored the covenant with God. 'Creation has been misused and we face threats to the balance of life, a growing ecological crisis and the effects of climate change. These are signs of our disordered relations with God, with one another and with creation, and we confess that they dishonour God's gift of life' (World Council of Churches, 10th Assembly, 2013).

'O God of the poor, help us to rescue the abandoned and forgotten of the
earth, who are so precious in your eyes,
God of love, show us our place in this world as channels of your love
for all the creatures of this earth,
God of mercy, may we receive your forgiveness and convey your mercy
throughout our common home.
Praise be to you! Amen'
(Pope Francis).

NICK READ

Unclean creatures

'Every creature that moves along the ground is to be regarded as unclean; it is not to be eaten. You are not to eat any creature that moves along the ground, whether it moves on its belly or walks on all fours or on many feet; it is unclean. Do not defile yourselves by any of these creatures. Do not make yourselves unclean by means of them or be made unclean by them. I am the Lord your God; consecrate yourselves and be holy, because I am holy. Do not make yourselves unclean by any creature that moves along the ground. I am the Lord, who brought you up out of Egypt to be your God; therefore be holy, because I am holy.'

Leviticus categorises living creatures as clean and unclean. For the latter, other translations use the words 'detestable' and 'abomination'. The harshness of the language grates with us – what makes an animal an abomination? As we have already seen, being unclean does not imply that God has no care for the animal; it is included within the covenant blessings. The lion (an unclean beast) is celebrated within the scriptures for its strength and majesty and used as a description of the kings of Israel.

The anthropologist Mary Douglas suggests that the language is meant as a warning – to the reader. It is not that the animal is detestable in itself, but that it becomes detestable to us because in handling it we will violate the demands of the covenant by touching something that is unclean. We can argue, for example, that cannibalism is an abomination but we don't blame the person being eaten!

What would it mean if humanity obeyed this stricture and left these creatures alone? The answer would be their complete ecological protection – there would be no economic exploitation of their meat or skins, just the ability for these animals to do what God intended them to do when he blessed them to become fruitful, increase in numbers and fill the earth (Genesis 1:22).

'Whoever has ears to hear, let them hear' (Mark 4:9, NIV).

NICK READ

Mary, mother of Jesus

Training as a Methodist preacher conditioned my approach to Bible study. I was urged to ask, 'Where is the good news in this?' and build a bridge between the gospel's eternal truths and contemporary life's changing circumstances. The Methodist Church's symbol is a cross within a circle – the cross that stands while the world revolves (also the Carthusian monastic order's motto – *stat crux dum volvitur orbis*).

So in exploring and considering Mary the mother of Jesus, I am looking for the links and connections between her and us, the ways our modern-day calling resonates with hers. Mary, visited by angels, risking everything, brave and full of faith – what has she to say to us in the 21st century?

Since the high Middle Ages, that has been Mary's particular role. She is the person with whom ordinary believers can identify in seeking to be drawn close to Jesus. Back in those days, as the church flourished and spread, it gradually traded spiritual power for political control. Fear of hell gives religious leaders opportunity for domination, and some took it. Participation in the Eucharist and access to God's forgiveness and grace belonged to the priestly hierarchy. At that time in church history, Mary became of great importance to ordinary believers. They recognised in her, a simple laywoman, a blueprint for faith that did not rely on priestly dispensation. She carried Jesus in her body; she held him in her arms; she fed him from her breasts. Nobody ever got closer to Jesus. In this, believers through the ages have found hope. She represents not dogma and orthodoxy, but personal and living faith.

Jesus, come close to us as you did to Mary, that our lives may bring you to birth in this fallen world. Amen

PENELOPE WILCOCK

Thresholds

In the sixth month the angel Gabriel was sent by God to a town in Galilee called Nazareth, to a virgin engaged to a man whose name was Joseph, of the house of David. The virgin's name was Mary. And he came to her and said, 'Greetings, favoured one! The Lord is with you.' But she was much perplexed by his words and pondered what sort of greeting this might be.

Theologians debate whether Mary's permission was required for the incarnation to happen. Most commentators incline to the view that God does what he likes and doesn't need to ask. Some scholars seem distinctly uneasy with the idea of God asking Mary if this could go ahead – particularly those anxious to ensure Mary is given no especially elevated religious status.

But in the spiritual realm, there is a law that nothing may cross a threshold without permission. In the letter to the Ephesians (4:27), we are urged to give the devil no foothold by the way we live – unless we invite evil in, it can have no part in us. In his farewell discourse in John's gospel (14:30), Jesus speaks of the ruler of this world (Satan) as having nothing on him – no hold over him, no claim on him. In the story of the Passover (Exodus 12), the blood of the sacrificial lamb is smeared on the lintel of the homes of God's people, denying access to the angel of death. Most importantly, Jesus describes himself in relation to us as standing patiently and courteously at our door, knocking to be admitted (Revelation 3:20), seeking fellowship with us.

God seeking Mary's permission is not so much an indication of her high spiritual status as consistent with how God always works and how he designed life to be. Boundaries, respect – these are holy. A Christian is called to be the servant, but not the doormat, of others.

May my dealings with others reflect your dealings with me, patient and courteous God. Yet even as I consider where my boundary lines should be drawn, let me say my door will always, always stand open to you. Amen

PENELOPE WILCOCK

Questions

[The shepherds] hurried off and found Mary and Joseph, and the baby, who was lying in the manger. When they had seen him, they spread the word concerning what had been told them about this child, and all who heard it were amazed at what the shepherds said to them. But Mary treasured up all these things and pondered them in her heart.

'How will this be,' Mary had asked the angel, 'since I am a virgin?' (Luke 1:34, NIV). Life can be downright confusing! We may not know our calling and may be unable to discern the contribution we make to the human race. So often I've wished Jesus stood physically here to explain what he wants of me, or which of a number of options he'd like me to pick.

How interesting, then, to see that even when an angel shows up in your back garden and tells you in your own mother tongue what God is asking of you, it's still completely baffling. 'What?' says Mary. 'How on earth…?'

In 1903, the poet Rainer Maria Rilke corresponded with a young protégé. In one letter, he said, 'I want to beg you, as much as I can, dear sir, to be patient towards all that is unsolved in your heart and to try to love the questions themselves like locked rooms and like books that are written in a very foreign tongue. Do not now seek the answers, which cannot be given you because you would not be able to live them. And the point is, to live everything. Live the questions now. Perhaps you will then gradually, without noticing it, live along some distant day into the answer.'

The presence of Jesus arrived as an unsolved question in Mary's life. At times she worried about him, got her timing wrong, even thought he might be mentally ill; and she received his broken body from the cross. When we walk the path of faith in chronic bewilderment, we have a travelling companion in Mary.

Beloved Lord, give me the faith I need to trust you.
Lead me when the way ahead is unclear. Let me not go astray. Amen

PENELOPE WILCOCK

Theotokos

The angel said to her, 'Do not be afraid, Mary, you have found favour with God. You will conceive and give birth to a son, and you are to call him Jesus. He will be great and will be called the Son of the Most High. The Lord God will give him the throne of his father David, and he will reign over Jacob's descendants for ever; his kingdom will never end.'

In the Orthodox Church, Mary and the icons depicting her with the infant Jesus are often referred to as *Theotokos*, Mother of God. The intense veneration of Mary that developed in the high Middle Ages began to be treated with suspicion and disapproval in the Protestant churches, who thought it unsuitable to draw attention away from the person of Christ. There was a danger, it was argued, that using the title *Theotokos* gave Mary a status equal to, or even exceeding, that of Jesus.

But, like it or not, there's no getting round it. If we believe Jesus is part of the Godhead, the second person of the Trinity, the Christ, the *logos*, divine as much as human, then Mary was the mother of God.

As Elizabeth says, 'Why am I so favoured, that the mother of my Lord should come to me?' (v. 43, NIV). Mary's status, however, is exclusively dependent upon Christ – it is the presence of Jesus that makes Mary holy, just as we are made holy by his indwelling Spirit in us.

Orthodox icons showing the death of Mary depict an adult, bearded Christ receiving into his hands her soul – which takes the form of a little child. And so is the circle made complete. This is all about holiness, humility and love.

Lord Jesus, as you came to dwell in Mary, filling her with the radiance of your Spirit, so dwell in me. Illumine my whole being by your grace present in my soul's deepest core. Amen

PENELOPE WILCOCK

Christ-bearer

The angel answered, 'The Holy Spirit will come on you, and the power of the Most High will overshadow you. So the holy one to be born will be called the Son of God. Even Elizabeth your relative is going to have a child in her old age, and she who was said to be unable to conceive is in her sixth month. For no word from God will ever fail.'

A favourite term for Mary is 'Christ-bearer' – the one who nurtures Jesus in the secret, hidden place of her womb. We can quickly see this calling is for us all. As the apostle Paul puts it, 'We have this treasure in jars of clay to show that this all-surpassing power is from God and not from us' (2 Corinthians 4:7, NIV). Like lanterns holding and sheltering the candle's living flame, we have the chance to enfold and embrace his presence, so it shines from us and through us, making us beautiful as his glory radiates from our lives.

But there's more than this. Mary literally grows Jesus, from the seed of the Spirit and the ordinary stuff of herself. In her, he can develop, getting ready to be born. In us, too, Christ's presence is not static and separate; he dwells within us in intimate inter-being with who we are and what we think, choose and do. His chance to grow and develop and mature in us depends on the environment we offer him. Healthy or toxic? Fed and rested or stressed and overwhelmed? Mary's responsibility was not only to him but also to herself, and this is true of us too.

And, then, Mary is the one who gives birth to him – the one who brings Jesus into the world where he can be seen and known. The first aim of the Third Order of Franciscans is 'To make the Lord Jesus Christ known and loved everywhere'; that is, we like Mary are called to deliver Christ safely out of our own bodies, where we have nurtured him, into a lost world still hungry to know his salvation.

'O come to my heart, Lord Jesus; there is room in my heart for thee'
(E.S. Elliot, 1864).

PENELOPE WILCOCK

Fiat

'I am the Lord's servant,' Mary answered. 'May your word to me be fulfilled.' Then the angel left her.

In the beginning when God created the heavens and the earth, the earth was a formless void and darkness covered the face of the deep, while a wind from God swept over the face of the waters. Then God said, 'Let there be light'; and there was light.

Creation starts when God says, 'Let there be light.' In Latin, this is *'Fiat lux'*. In the Latin translation of Luke's account of the angel's visit to Mary, Mary's response to his message uses the same word: *'Fiat mihi'* – 'Let it be unto me.' As God's *fiat* begins the creation of the earth, Mary's *fiat* begins a new creation.

This word is no limp or half-hearted acquiescence. Meaning 'Let it become' or 'It will become', *fiat* is an order or a decree. In modern society, we have the example of fiat money (which all our money now is), currency spoken or decreed into being. Its value is the authority it represents, not an inherent value of gold reserves.

So *fiat* implies authority to create something, but it also has a quality of enthusiasm and eagerness. Not 'Oh, all right, then,' but 'Go for it!' In this case, Mary's eager permission also shines with humility and obedience – 'let it be with me according to your word.'

At this moment of receiving the angel's message; when she later hears a sword will pierce her heart (Luke 2:35); when a young Jesus takes off to the temple (Luke 2:41–51); when Mary instructs the servants, 'Do whatever he tells you,' at the wedding at Cana (John 2:5, NRSV); when she keeps watch at the foot of the cross (John 19:25) – her *fiat* had consequences, as all our *fiats* do. What we set in motion goes a long way down the road, and we can't even see round the first bend.

Take my hand and lead me, Lord. Give me faith to begin and courage to persevere. From this moment, clear through to the moment I die, may I walk with you, serve you, keep faith with you. Amen

PENELOPE WILCOCK

The Lord's doula

Mary got ready and hurried to... Zechariah's home and greeted Elizabeth. When Elizabeth heard Mary's greeting, the baby leaped in her womb, and Elizabeth was filled with the Holy Spirit. In a loud voice she exclaimed: 'Blessed are you among women, and blessed is the child you will bear!... As soon as the sound of your greeting reached my ears, the baby in my womb leaped for joy.'

The Greek words of Mary's response to the angel's message, 'Behold the handmaid of the Lord' (Luke 1:38, KJV), are *doulā kyrie* – the Lord's doula.

A doula was a personal servant who kept close companionship with the one served, waiting upon them. There's also a special resonance with childbirth – a doula is someone who comes to stay with a woman close to giving birth, helping her in all kinds of practical ways at the end of her pregnancy and when she has a new baby.

The angel not only told Mary of her own pregnancy but also gave her news of her cousin Elizabeth, herself a few weeks away from giving birth.

Mary received the news, taking it all in carefully, and responded, 'Here I am, the Lord's doula! Let's go for it!' She sets off without delay to see Elizabeth, with whom 'Mary stayed about three months... and then went back home' (Luke 1:56, GNT). So Mary acts as the Lord's doula for her cousin, as well as offering herself in humility as the Lord's personal servant. She is both there to wait upon him, and there to wait upon others in his name.

When she arrives at Elizabeth's home, an astonishing four-way spiritual encounter takes place both mothers and both unborn children full of the Holy Spirit, recognising the significance and power of what is happening; nothing less than the incarnation of God's chosen Messiah. This meeting is resonant with holiness and overflows with joy.

By your grace, dearest Lord, may I discern the area of service right for me.
May I listen for your voice, hear your call, then in eager faith carry out
what you ask me to do. Amen

PENELOPE WILCOCK

The power of praise

[Elizabeth exclaimed:] 'Blessed is she who has believed that the Lord would fulfil his promises to her!' And Mary said: 'My soul glorifies the Lord and my spirit rejoices in God my Saviour, for he has been mindful of the humble state of his servant. From now on all generations will call me blessed, for the Mighty One has done great things for me – holy is his name.'

Statues and pictures of the Virgin Mary almost invariably depict someone meek, demure and docile. I don't think so! Her reactions are interesting. When the angel visited her, she listened carefully and had the presence of mind to ask questions. Then, rather than withdrawing to a private space to worry about how she would cope, she sets off striding across country to seek spiritual alliance with Elizabeth, and offer her support through childbirth. The Holy Spirit element of their meeting could be measured on the Richter scale, and the Spirit sets Mary off into the mother of all praise and political protest songs. The Magnificat is a model of how to pray God's power into a situation – announcing change as though it has already happened. In a social scenario showing no evidence whatsoever of the changes for which she praises God, Mary's faith rings out clearly. God has done this. However long we have to wait for it, whatever our material circumstances suggest to the contrary, this is God's will and it shall be.

For both these women, history ground on relentlessly. John the Baptist was beheaded and Jesus was crucified. Even so, we know their faith had good foundation. They built on the rock of God's promises, and their confidence was surely not in vain.

Every single one of us faces events in life that make us quail and doubt and reduce us to jelly. In such times, if we close our eyes, perhaps we can imagine Mary and Elizabeth, standing on the track leading to Elizabeth's house, and Mary's song ringing out: 'My soul doth magnify the Lord!' (v. 46, KJV).

God of all power, instil in me the faith that was in Mary and Elizabeth, to trust unfailingly in your holy name. Amen

PENELOPE WILCOCK

Advocate for justice

'[The Lord's] name is holy; from one generation to another he shows mercy to those who honour him. He has stretched out his mighty arm and scattered the proud with all their plans. He has brought down mighty kings from their thrones, and lifted up the lowly. He has filled the hungry with good things, and sent the rich away with empty hands.'

An arresting aspect of Mary's song of praise is that it looks outward from her personal circumstances to wider concerns. If Mary were a character in a work of fiction, her song would not read like this. We might expect her focus to be on the privilege of her position and its perils. It would be reasonable for her to be wrapped up in what this means for her, why God chose her in particular, how she would cope with childbirth and what she would say to Joseph. Apparently that's not at all on Mary's mind. As the Holy Spirit moves in her and Elizabeth and their unborn children, the praise song that bursts forth from her has a very different focus.

There's a long tradition that religion and politics don't mix – that preachers should steer clear of directing the political inclinations of their congregations. But this song of Mary, in line with all the Old Testament prophets, takes an entirely different tack. The coming of the Messiah is not, for Mary, primarily a matter of personal piety and inward spiritual journey, but is socially and politically manifest.

Clear in Mary's song – and in every one of the biblical prophets – is the obligation of the people of God to work and speak up for social justice, to advocate for the poor and marginalised. The coming of the kingdom is squarely evidenced in the extent to which the hungry are fed, the naked clothed, the vulnerable supported and the lives of the rich – that would be us – radically simplified.

God of the poor and dispossessed, who led your people in the wilderness,
who hears the prayers of the homeless and cares for the plight of the poor,
shape us in your likeness, that your kingdom may come on earth. Amen

PENELOPE WILCOCK

The unending story

'[The Lord] has helped his servant Israel, remembering to be merciful to Abraham and his descendants for ever, just as he promised our ancestors.'

The Lord said to Moses, 'Tell Aaron and his sons, "This is how you are to bless the Israelites. Say to them: 'The Lord bless you and keep you; the Lord make his face shine on you and be gracious to you; the Lord turn his face towards you and give you peace.'"'

Mary is sometimes called the first disciple. To her, before anyone else, the angel announced that the watched-for, longed-for Messiah had arrived. In her his presence is physically manifest. Through Mary he incarnates. This is the calling of every disciple of Jesus – to know the indwelling power of the presence of God alive and active; to carry and bring forth the only-begotten Son of God into the world he came to save.

But salvation history has deep roots. The Bible story goes back to the creation of the world – even to before time began. Mary identifies this momentous occasion as one part of a chain of events stretching back through the generations; she can see God's blessing and *shalom* through his watching over and guiding of his people through exile and exodus, through desert journeying, through good times and bad.

By the same token, salvation history stretches forward. What began before a word of scripture was written, and shines through the pages of the Bible, rolls forward into the living out of the gospel in our day-to-day lives. Five minutes of watching the news makes it abundantly clear God's intervention in human affairs is not complete. The world has never been more urgently in need of his salvation, of repentance and obedience to his will and ways. The story is not done. As the willingness of Abraham and Moses and Mary were needed, so is our willingness needed for the present day. The story is not yet over, but the end is assured.

Thank you for opening the way of salvation to us in Jesus. By your grace may we be the signposts for our generation, our lives pointing out faithfully your true and trustworthy path. Amen

PENELOPE WILCOCK

'Do not be afraid'

'Do not let your hearts be troubled. You believe in God; believe also in me… I am in my Father, and you are in me, and I am in you… Peace I leave with you; my peace I give you. I do not give to you as the world gives. Do not let your hearts be troubled and do not be afraid.'

Seeing his message had troubled and disturbed Mary, the angel said: 'Do not be afraid, Mary, you have found favour with God' (Luke 1:30, NIV). This greeting – 'Do not be afraid' – recurs throughout the Bible. It's one of the ways Jesus reveals God to us. When the disciples blanched in terror as he came walking across the water, Jesus called out: 'Don't be afraid – it's me!' (Matthew 14:27). When he begins to say goodbye to them (John 14), Jesus reminds them to take courage and not be afraid. And at the annunciation of Jesus' birth, the angel reassured Mary that she need not be afraid.

There's a paradox in this. On the one hand, the manifestation of God's presence inspires awe so deep it feels like fear. A burning bush, a host of angels, a human being walking on the sea, the announcement of pregnancy to a young virgin, the unexpected revelation that salvation comes only through terrible suffering – the ways of God perturb us, challenging our expectations and unsettling our assumptions.

On the other hand, God's 'Do not be afraid' is not an ineffectual emollient. Just as when God said, 'Let there be light,' it set off the Big Bang, so when he says, 'Do not be afraid,' peace and courage arise in the heart. Mary transformed from an apprehensive young woman into a prophetess – her 'Fiat!' ringing with confidence because God's power and presence were spoken into the depths of her listening heart.

'Do not be afraid' is God's calling card; peace, the sign of his presence.

Speak to my heart, too, Spirit of power and peace. Give me the faith I need to walk steadily through this troubled world, holding high the unwavering light of the gospel's flame. Amen

PENELOPE WILCOCK

Overshadowing

Whoever dwells in the shelter of the Most High will rest in the shadow of the Almighty. I will say of the Lord, 'He is my refuge and my fortress, my God, in whom I trust.' Surely he will save you from the fowler's snare and from the deadly pestilence. He will cover you with his feathers, and under his wings you will find refuge.

In his *Godly Play* (1995), a gloriously comprehensive exploration of the Christian faith and tradition through storytelling, Jerome Berryman uses repeated actions and phrases to flag up links between different Bible stories. In his script about Abraham's journey into the desert, Berryman brings out the courage that was needed to venture beyond the boundaries of the familiar, because gods were local and Abraham had not yet tested the possibility that God would still be with him in unknown territory. Berryman writes of Abraham setting out alone into that barren and shifting landscape under the stars, and the *Godly Play* storyteller bends low over the tiny wooden Abraham figure in the sand of the desert box, cupping protective hands around its vulnerability, telling how God came very close to Abraham, and Abraham came very close to God, in that wilderness of sand dunes and stars.

In the same way Mary, when she accepted the call to be the one who bore Christ in her body, stepped beyond human familiarity into unexplored territory – dangerous, threatening, otherwise entirely mysterious. She asked, 'How can this be?' (Luke 1:34, NRSV). She was both puzzled and apprehensive. And the angel told her the power of the Most High would overshadow her. God would come very close to Mary, and Mary would come very close to God, as she set out on this daring and lonely adventure.

This heady mixture of mystery, courage and trust is central to every miracle, every transformative act of grace in human life. It is the invitation held out to everyone who is born, and is born again. The power of the Most High overshadows our whispered 'Yes.' God goes with us.

Lead me, then, into the unknown, and I will follow. I trust more than I fear, for without you I am nothing. Overshadow me. Amen

PENELOPE WILCOCK

'No word from God will ever fail'

'There will be signs in the sun, moon and stars... the heavenly bodies will be shaken... when you see these things happening, you know that the kingdom of God is near. Truly I tell you, this generation will certainly not pass away until all these things have happened. Heaven and earth will pass away, but my words will never pass away.'

Telling Mary of Elizabeth's pregnancy, the angel said, 'No word from God will ever fail' (Luke 1:37, NIV). But other translations render this as 'There is nothing that God cannot do' (GNT) and 'Nothing will be impossible with God' (NRSV). It can be puzzling when different translations don't seem to be the same as each other at all.

The Greek word used – *rhema* – can mean either 'thing' or 'word' (in the sense of an utterance or saying, rather than a single word). The verb *adunateo* means 'to be weak' or 'to be powerless' when applied to people, or 'to be impossible' when applied to things. The King James translation incorrectly joins 'no' to 'thing', resulting in 'nothing shall be impossible'. The right sense of the Greek is that what God says or does can never be ineffectual or powerless.

This means that God can be absolutely trusted. Even when circumstances make our faith falter – as Peter's did when he began to walk across the sea to Jesus – it is what God does and says we should trust, nothing else.

This was so important for Mary. She was asked to accept a pregnancy that would shake her relationships with Joseph and her family; to accept being the mother to someone whose life attracted turbulence and persecution. It must have meant everything to hold in her heart the memory of an angel standing before her, reminding her that whatever (thing or word) proceeds from God will always achieve its purpose. It will not fail. And this is true for all our own circumstances as well.

I am yours, O God, and you will never fail me.
By your grace may I trust in you for ever. Amen

PENELOPE WILCOCK

Mary returned to her home

My people are bent on turning away from me. To the Most High they call… How can I give you up, Ephraim? How can I hand you over, O Israel?… [H]is children shall come trembling from the west. They shall come trembling like birds from Egypt, and like doves from the land of Assyria; and I will return them to their homes, says the Lord.

After she visited Elizabeth, staying until Elizabeth's baby was born, Mary returned to her home. The Bible has a number of stories about leaving home and then returning home: Jesus' parable of the prodigal son (Luke 15:1–32); the Gerasene demoniac (Mark 5:1–20) whom Jesus heals; and the disciples going back from Jerusalem to Galilee after Jesus' death and resurrection are some examples. The Old Testament also carries big themes of exodus and exile. 'Let my people go!' cried Moses (Exodus 10:3), and 'How shall we sing the Lord's song in a strange land?' (Psalm 137:4, KJV) lamented the people of God in captivity.

In these stories, there are two sides to the coin of what home might mean. On the one hand, it is a place of belonging and, for the exiles, intense yearning. On the other hand, it is a place of challenge and confrontation: 'Prophets are not without honour, except in their hometown, and among their own kin, and in their own house,' said Jesus (Mark 6:4, NRSV). For Mary returning home after her visit to Elizabeth there was a sense of apprehension. She left the company of an ally who understood, returning with her inexplicable pregnancy to face Joseph, her parents, her neighbours.

But these Bible stories of leaving home and returning home are about spiritual growth and transformation. Like the prodigal son, like Moses, like the Easter disciples, Mary went back home different because of the journey she had made. Things would not be easy, yet Mary shone with the assurance of unshakeable faith.

God of light and hope, dancing in creation, calling me on, give me courage and faith like Mary's to travel where your Spirit beckons. I put my trust in you. Amen

PENELOPE WILCOCK

His mother's son

[Jesus said:] 'The Spirit of the Lord is on me, because he has anointed me to proclaim good news to the poor. He has sent me to proclaim freedom for the prisoners and recovery of sight for the blind, to set the oppressed free, to proclaim the year of the Lord's favour.' Then he rolled up the scroll, gave it back to the attendant and sat down.

Jesus stood to deliver the reading, but the implication of him handing back the scroll and sitting down is that he is about to deliver the sermon. Luke continues this story of Jesus in the synagogue at Capernaum, saying, 'The eyes of everyone in the synagogue were fastened on him' (v. 20b, NIV). Evidently Jesus had a considerable reputation among these people who knew him well. Luke continues, 'He began by saying to them, "Today this scripture is fulfilled in your hearing"' (v. 21, NIV).

The first creed of the church was 'Jesus is Lord.' He is the centre around which the Christian faith developed. This does not displace God the Father or God the Holy Spirit, because Jesus is the means through which the Father is revealed to us and the Spirit comes to us. But in Christianity, Jesus holds the unique central place. There is no one like him. In him is all scripture fulfilled.

Even so, Jesus is not without a context. He had a home and it shaped him. He had a mother and she brought him up. Joseph passes through the gospel story without saying anything at all – and this is an icon to us, of the living Word fostered and nurtured by silence. But Mary asked questions, declared faith and sang. And the words of her song of praise and political protest are arrestingly similar to these words with which Jesus announces the start of his preaching and teaching ministry. He is good to go. She has taught him well. She steps back now and lets him shine.

In my life, too, Lord Jesus, may you have first place. By word and action may I echo your priority and Mary's – the good news of God for the poor and marginalised everywhere. Amen

PENELOPE WILCOCK

Christmas with Luke

Almost everyone knows the story of the first Christmas – the wise men, the baby in the manger, the shepherds and, of course, the innkeeper who turned Mary and Joseph away. There are two accounts in the gospels of the birth of Jesus (in Matthew and Luke). They agree that Jesus was born in Bethlehem, that his mother was Mary and her husband was Joseph, but there are no 'wise men' or guiding star in Luke, no shepherds or manger in Matthew (and there is no innkeeper in either of them!).

The reason for these differences seems to lie in the fundamental purpose of the two authors. Matthew's preoccupation, here and all through his gospel, is to demonstrate that the life and significance of Jesus flow from the prophecies of the Hebrew scriptures. Jesus' birth was no accident but a fulfilment of a long-term purpose of God. In Matthew's brief account of the nativity, Old Testament prophecies are quoted six times.

Luke, on the other hand, tells us in his preface what his objective is: to set out as accurately as possible the whole story of the life of Jesus the Messiah. He is offering, he says, an 'orderly account' of it, based on the evidence of 'eyewitnesses' (Luke 1:2–3, NRSV). For Luke, it is important to tell the story precisely as it has been handed down. Among those eyewitnesses, I suggest, might well have been Mary herself. After the resurrection, reliable tradition tells us, she went to live with the apostle John at Ephesus, in the same part of the world (modern Turkey) as Luke himself came from. Whether at first or second hand, she was an indispensable eyewitness. Certainly she is the only possible source of much of the story of the nativity, and of her wonderment at her own role in it.

A distinguished atheist was asked on BBC Radio 4 last year about what he had done over Christmas. He said he'd gone to the midnight Eucharist. 'Why?' 'Because this is the most beautiful story ever told, and I don't want it to be forgotten.' So let us, who believe, now soak ourselves in the wonderful story of the Word made flesh – a story that is very old, but always new.

DAVID WINTER

The dawn from on high

'And you, child, will be called the prophet of the Most High; for you will go before the Lord to prepare his ways, to give knowledge of salvation to his people by the forgiveness of their sins. By the tender mercy of our God, the dawn from on high will break upon us, to give light to those who sit in darkness and in the shadow of death, to guide our feet into the way of peace.' The child grew and became strong in spirit, and he was in the wilderness until the day he appeared publicly to Israel.

First, the forerunner. Luke's story of the birth of Jesus begins in the temple in Jerusalem, where an elderly priest, Zechariah, was ministering at the altar of incense. An angel appeared to him and said that his wife Elizabeth, who was 'barren… and getting on in years' (v. 7, NRSV), would have a son. The child, to be called John, would be 'great' (v. 15, NRSV), and 'make ready a people prepared for the Lord' (v. 17, NRSV). Our reading today is part of Zechariah's outburst of praise at the birth of the child, duly named John and known to us as John the Baptist.

The priest had been struck dumb during his wife's pregnancy, because he questioned the angel's promise, but here he is full of joy. The 'Dayspring from on high' (v. 78, KJV) will come, and his son will herald that coming. For long centuries the Jewish people had waited for their Messiah, and that longing had reached fever pitch – three centuries of occupation by Greece and then the Romans had created a desperate desire for God to intervene. It was about to happen, but not at all in the way they had anticipated. Angelic forces were at work, as Elizabeth already knew, and a son of David would be born, but his coming would be good news for 'all the people' (2:10, NRSV), including Romans and Greeks. And although he would be 'born king' (Matthew 2:2, NRSV), he would not be born in a palace.

For long centuries the people had waited and hoped. At times the darkness had seemed impenetrable. But now a new dawn was promised.

'The light shines in the darkness…' (John 1:5, NRSV).

DAVID WINTER

Here I am, Lord

The angel said to her, 'Do not be afraid, Mary, for you have found favour with God. And now, you will conceive in your womb and bear a son, and you will name him Jesus. He will be great, and will be called the Son of the Most High, and the Lord God will give to him the throne of his ancestor David. He will reign over the house of Jacob forever, and of his kingdom there will be no end.' Mary said to the angel, 'How can this be, since I am a virgin?' The angel said to her, 'The Holy Spirit will come upon you, and the power of the Most High will overshadow you; therefore the child to be born will be holy; he will be called Son of God'… Then Mary said, 'Here am I, the servant of the Lord; let it be with me according to your word.'

This is the perfect reading for Christmas Eve, as we await in our imaginations the hour when Mary will give birth – surely the most important event since the creation. At the centre of it all is this young woman, with her carpenter husband beside her, bedded down in a stable in the crowded small town of Bethlehem. It all follows from her simple, trusting response to the words of the angel Gabriel: 'Here am I, the servant of the Lord; let it be with me according to your word.'

The angel called Mary 'highly favoured' (v. 28, NIV) – 'full of grace', as some translations put it. She has not been chosen for the role of mother of the Messiah because of her experience or maternal qualities – she is probably a teenager. What matters is her faithful obedience. Of course, the angel's message is a shock. Of course, she can't comprehend the full implications of his words. Yet we see it again and again: God doesn't make mistakes. Those he calls, he enables. And this young woman is eventually revealed as wise beyond her years and the perfect mother for the incarnate Son of God.

Those words, 'Here am I,' took Mary, as they have countless others down the Christian centuries, into unimaginable realms of joyful if sacrificial fulfilment.

DAVID WINTER

Once in royal David's city

In those days a decree went out from Emperor Augustus that all the world should be registered... All went to their own towns to be registered. Joseph also went from the town of Nazareth in Galilee to Judea, to the city of David called Bethlehem, because he was descended from the house and family of David. He went to be registered with Mary, to whom he was engaged and who was expecting a child. While they were there, the time came for her to deliver her child. And she gave birth to her firstborn son and wrapped him in bands of cloth, and laid him in a manger, because there was no place for them in the inn.

Here is the heart of the Christmas narrative: the census, the journey to Bethlehem (60 miles and probably no 'little donkey'), Mary nearing the end of her pregnancy. Mary and Joseph take perhaps a couple of weeks on the road, enjoying hospitality in the towns and villages they pass through. And then, when they finally get to Bethlehem, the 'inn' is full, so that they have to find overnight accommodation in what appears to be a stable.

Rulers and their deputies in the Roman world loved counting heads, mainly to make sure that they collected taxes – a trait not unknown today. But Joseph may have been keen anyway to go to Bethlehem, to establish his own family roots as a descendant of King David. Maybe the long journey brings it on, but it seems that very soon after arriving and settling in their temporary accommodation, Mary goes into labour and gives birth to the promised son. Doubtless she has prepared a convenient feeding trough as a temporary crib, and the Son of God is laid in it. His first cries, signalling the opening of his little lungs, echo around the stable walls.

Thus the angelic word is fulfilled. Mary and Joseph are 'engaged' (Matthew 1:18, NRSV), which means that they have not yet had sexual intercourse. The baby's mother is Mary, making him truly human; his 'father' is the Holy Spirit (Luke 1:35), making him truly divine.

'Veiled in flesh the Godhead see,' we shall sing in 'Hark! The Herald Angels Sing'. That was what Mary and Joseph saw, in a feeding trough, 2,000 years ago.

DAVID WINTER

And there were shepherds

In that region there were shepherds living in the fields, keeping watch over their flock by night. Then an angel of the Lord stood before them, and the glory of the Lord shone around them, and they were terrified. But the angel said to them, 'Do not be afraid; for see – I am bringing you good news of great joy for all the people: to you is born this day in the city of David a Saviour, who is the Messiah, the Lord. This will be a sign for you: you will find a child wrapped in bands of cloth and lying in a manger.' And suddenly there was with the angel a multitude of the heavenly host, praising God and saying, 'Glory to God in the highest heaven, and on earth peace among those whom he favours!'

Luke, the great storyteller, now almost casually introduces a surprise element in the narrative: 'And there were shepherds.' He changes the focus with the single word 'and'. (The translators tidy it up and miss the drama.) Why suddenly shepherds? A moment ago we were in the stable with Mary, Joseph and a newborn baby – the Son of God, no less. The answer is, because this event needs witnesses. And the chosen witnesses are a group of scruffy, smelly shepherds bedding down with their sheep on the hills above Bethlehem. Shepherds have an honourable role in the Bible, from shepherd-boy David to the unforgettable claim of the psalmist that 'The Lord is my shepherd' (Psalm 23:1). Despite the biblical imagery, however, their role was not highly regarded – they were socially isolated and couldn't get to the synagogue or the temple.

But they are the ones chosen to receive this momentous angelic announcement: 'to you is born this day... a Saviour, who is the Messiah, the Lord.' They are invited to go down to the town and see this wonder, and given a 'sign' to ensure they find the right baby. The sign – the baby will be lying in a feeding trough ('manger' is simply too posh, I feel) – must surprise them. This was a Saviour for people like them.

The 'peace' of which the angels speak is not ours but God's.
This is his gift to us.

DAVID WINTER

Words to treasure

When the angels had left them and gone into heaven, the shepherds said to one another, 'Let us go now to Bethlehem and see this thing that has taken place, which the Lord has made known to us.' So they went with haste and found Mary and Joseph, and the child lying in the manger. When they saw this, they made known what had been told them about this child; and all who heard it were amazed at what the shepherds told them. But Mary treasured all these words and pondered them in her heart. The shepherds returned, glorifying and praising God for all they had heard and seen, as it had been told them.

What the angels told the shepherds was very specific, not only about what had happened, but also about its meaning. This is the birth of a baby who is Saviour, Messiah and Lord. In the context of the history of the people of Israel, that certainly was, as the shepherds were told, 'good news of great joy' (v. 10, NRSV). After all those centuries of alien occupation, the tide, it seems, has turned. The long-promised Messiah has been born. It is not quite how they, or anyone else, envisaged it, but they hurry to the town to see for themselves. When the shepherds reach the stable, they discover that it is all exactly as they were told. It seems that their arrival attracts a crowd ('all who heard it'), who are suitably 'amazed'.

Only Mary, who of course knew much of this nine months earlier, is able quietly to absorb its full significance. The 'but' is important. In contrast to the hubbub of excitement, the mother of the Messiah holds her baby son, treasures the moment and ponders the angelic words in her heart. I love this image of Mary – 'pondering' is a lovely word, with its implication of giving due weight to ideas and events. At this moment her simple act of faith is vindicated and her joy is complete.

This ancient prayer from the Catholic rosary seems very appropriate:
'Hail Mary, full of grace. Blessed are you among women,
and blessed is the fruit of your womb, Jesus.'

DAVID WINTER

Jesus is his name

After eight days had passed, it was time to circumcise the child; and he was called Jesus, the name given by the angel before he was conceived in the womb. When the time came for their purification according to the law of Moses, they brought him up to Jerusalem to present him to the Lord (as it is written in the law of the Lord, 'Every firstborn male shall be designated as holy to the Lord'), and they offered a sacrifice according to what is stated in the law of the Lord, 'a pair of turtledoves or two young pigeons.'

This reading describes the three birth ceremonies of Judaism. First, and most fundamental, is circumcision, the outward sign for males of being within God's covenant. That included the naming, and, as the angel had instructed Joseph, the baby was called Jesus. The name – Yeshua, or Joshua, in Hebrew – means 'saviour'.

Perhaps older readers will remember a chorus from my childhood from the *Golden Bells Hymn Book* (1925): 'He did not come to judge the world, he did not come to blame. He did not only come to seek, it was to save he came. And when we call him "Saviour" then we call him by his name.' It just about says it all, where the name is concerned!

Next there was purification (cleansing from the supposed stains of childbirth) and then presentation. That fulfilled the requirement that all 'firstfruits' should be offered to God – fish, fruit, grain and even offspring. The law required the parents of a firstborn male child to make a sacrificial offering in his place.

In this case, Mary and Joseph make the offering permitted for those who cannot afford a sheep or bullock – a pair of pigeons (Leviticus 12:8). That's a reminder that Jesus was born into a household of simplicity and poverty. No palaces, crowns or luxury, but an ordinary 'working-class' home in a despised town – 'Can anything good come out of Nazareth?' (John 1:46, NRSV). Yes, the best thing ever!

Jesus said he had come to seek out and to save the lost. Like his namesake, Joshua, he will rescue us and lead us to the promised land.

DAVID WINTER

My eyes have seen

Now there was a man in Jerusalem whose name was Simeon; this man was righteous and devout, looking forward to the consolation of Israel, and the Holy Spirit rested on him. It had been revealed to him by the Holy Spirit that he would not see death before he had seen the Lord's Messiah. Guided by the Spirit, Simeon came into the temple; and when the parents brought in the child Jesus, to do for him what was customary under the law, Simeon took him in his arms and praised God, saying, 'Master, now you are dismissing your servant in peace, according to your word; for my eyes have seen your salvation, which you have prepared in the presence of all peoples, a light for revelation to the Gentiles and for glory to your people Israel.'

Surely Luke's only source for the story of two elderly prophets in the temple was Mary. Here we have the man Simeon, who had been assured by the Holy Spirit that he would live to see the long-promised Messiah. Prompted by the Spirit, he is there when the holy family arrive for the presentation ritual. He bursts into a psalm of thanksgiving, which generations of Christians have known as the Nunc Dimittis. Its theme is a wonderful enlargement of the contemporary Jewish understanding of messiahship. The coming of this child, 'great David's greater Son',* would not only be glory for Israel, but also light for the Gentiles.

This extension of God's covenant to embrace every nation goes back to Abraham, of course (Genesis 18:18), but the Judaism of the time was more concerned with the fate and survival of Israel – a new warrior-king would be needed to bring it about. Jesus would prove to be many things – healer, prophet, redeemer, lamb of God – but definitely not a warrior!

Similarly, the prophet Anna has been longing for the Messiah-redeemer (vv. 36–38). She is 'of a great age' – 84. Here in the temple of God the age groups meet: the newborn baby, the young parents and two people tarrying in the departure lounge of life. And all are blessed.

Glory for Israel meant light for the Gentiles. Hallelujah!

* 'Hail to the Lord's Anointed' (James Montgomery, 1821).

DAVID WINTER

Mary's 'sword'

And the child's father and mother were amazed at what was being said about him. Then Simeon blessed them and said to his mother Mary, 'This child is destined for the falling and the rising of many in Israel, and to be a sign that will be opposed so that the inner thoughts of many will be revealed—and a sword will pierce your own soul too.'

It is the role of a prophet to speak the truth, welcome or unwelcome. Having proclaimed a beautiful hymn of praise for the birth of the Messiah, Simeon now has a few sombre words for the child's mother, Mary.

She, of all the people in the story, is profoundly conscious of the significance of the birth of Jesus. She can remember the angelic message, 'He… will be called the Son of the Most High' (Luke 1:32, NRSV). She knows that while he is certainly her son, Jesus is also the world's Saviour. She has 'treasured all these words and pondered them in her heart' (v. 19, NRSV).

Now the prophet reminds her that though Jesus is an 'ordinary' baby, he will be an extraordinary adult, with a unique and controversial impact. His message and his methods will profoundly disturb the Jewish people. For many, as the apostle Paul later observes, he will be a 'stumbling block' (1 Corinthians 1:23, NRSV), raising doubts about what they have been taught by the scribes and Pharisees. Some will heed his call and rise; some will reject it and fall. As the gospel story unfolds, we see how Jesus' message divides the crowds. Some believe and follow him; others cry 'Crucify him!' (Mark 15:13–14, NRSV).

'And a sword will pierce your own soul too.' That would surely have happened as Mary stood by the cross where her dear son was being cruelly executed. Perhaps only a mother can imagine precisely how that 'pierced' her soul.

And then the resurrection. Only Luke tells us that Mary was there in the upper room to be a witness of it, and to hear him talking of 'going to his Father' (and therefore leaving her). Glory, yes, for a needy world. But for the mother who had fed him at her breast, surely a sense of loss, too.

There is no such thing as a pain-free pilgrimage, but at the end all is grace.

DAVID WINTER

And the child grew

When [Jesus' parents] had finished everything required by the law of the Lord, they returned to Galilee, to their own town of Nazareth. The child grew and became strong, filled with wisdom; and the favour of God was upon him... And Jesus increased in wisdom and in years, and in divine and human favour.

These two brief summaries conclude Luke's narrative of the birth of Jesus. Apart from the story of Jesus going missing on a family pilgrimage to Jerusalem (vv. 41–50), which only Luke records, that is all we are reliably told about his childhood and early adult years until he is baptised by John in the Jordan and begins a brief public ministry that changes the history of the world. He is then, we are told, 'about thirty' (Luke 3:23).

In today's verses we have a tidying up of the narrative. The family return to Nazareth, where Jesus is to grow up. We would love to know more about his childhood (some of our children's hymns offer an unlikely picture of a 'meek and mild' child, which the incident in the temple seems to contradict). There are apocryphal stories of his childhood in later writings (the boy Jesus doing miracles, for instance), but historically speaking these are truly hidden years.

Luke tells us that the boy grows 'in wisdom and in stature' (v. 52; see NRSV footnote) and also in 'divine and human favour'. God loves his incarnate Son, and clearly people are also drawn to him, as they will be throughout his life. But we can assume that all of that is within the context of a normal childhood, though obviously in a devout and God-fearing home. He would learn to know and respect the scriptures and become familiar with the usual family and synagogue prayers. The teachers of the law in the temple are 'amazed' at his scriptural knowledge (v. 47, NRSV). This godly childhood helps prepare him for his later adult role.

The child becomes a man – indeed, as he liked to call himself,
the Son of Man, the perfect image of what God intended human beings
to be. The birth of the child was but the astonishing beginning of
'the greatest story ever told' (film title, 1965).

DAVID WINTER

This page is left blank for your notes

Reading *New Daylight* in a group

SALLY WELCH

I am aware that although some of you cherish the moments of quiet during the day that enable you to read and reflect on the passages we offer you in *New Daylight*, other readers prefer to study in small groups, to enable conversation and discussion and the sharing of insights. With this in mind, here are some ideas for discussion starters within a study group. Some of the questions are generic and can be applied to any set of contributions within this issue; others are specific to certain sets of readings. I hope they generate some interesting reflections and conversations!

General discussion starters

These questions can be used for any study series within this issue. Remember, there are no right or wrong answers; they are intended simply to enable a group to engage in conversation.

- What do you think the main idea or theme of the author is in this series? Do you think they succeeded in communicating this to you, or were you more interested in the side issues?

- Have you had any experience of the issues that are raised in the study? How have they affected your life?

- What evidence does the author use to support their ideas? Do they use personal observations and experience, facts, quotations from other authorities? Which appeals to you most?

- Does the author make a 'call to action'? Is that call realistic and achievable? Do you think their ideas will work in the secular world?

- Can you identify specific passages that struck you personally – as interesting, profound, difficult to understand or illuminating?

- Did you learn something new reading this series? Will you think differently about some things, and if so, what are they?

Mary, mother of Jesus (Penelope Wilcock)

'Mary – visited by angels, risking everything, brave and full of faith.' How does the life of Mary speak to you today? Do you agree that Mary's role as an 'ordinary person' is helpful in enabling believers to draw closer to

Jesus? Does the Magnificat still hold the power that it did as a blueprint for radical living?

Joshua 1—7 (Fiona Stratta)

In what ways is Joshua the 'ideal leader'? Which of his qualities would you most like to have? One of Joshua's roles is to remind the children of Israel of the goodness of God towards them. How do you remember God's goodness to you?

Reflection (Christmas in Luke, David Winter)

'The "peace" of which the angels speak is not ours but God's. This is his gift to us.'

'Glory to God in the highest heaven, and on earth peace among those whom he favours!'

Author profile: Debbie Orriss

What does your post as discipleship coordinator involve?

I coordinate the initial training for the authorised lay ministries in the diocese: lay pastoral assistant, lay worship leader and licensed lay minister (also known as readers). I do some teaching as part of this, which I love! I am also involved with enabling adults and young people to grow in and live out their faith.

Do you have a story about how you came to faith?

I was fortunate to grow up in a loving Christian home and enjoyed going to church and singing in the choir. I was confirmed at the age of 13 and felt a strong sense of God's presence as the bishop laid his hands on my head. At 16 my life was rocked by the sudden death of my dad. This raised major questions for me about God. Through the prayers of people in our church and many acts of kindness, my family got through this terrible time, and I realised that we were experiencing God's love despite what had happened.

My faith grew while I was at university and, following graduation, I taught in two primary schools. After about six years I began to feel restless and gradually realised that God was calling me to ministry as a Church Army evangelist and enabler of others in evangelism and discipleship. I'm still learning how to be a disciple, how to be a follower of Jesus.

Which authors have influenced you?

That's a really difficult question. I've been influenced by authors such as Henri Nouwen, Richard Rohr and Philip Yancey, and I had the privilege of meeting Desmond Tutu a few years ago. Jesus shines out of him, and I greatly admire his faith and wisdom.

Where do you meet God most frequently?

In creation. Being by the sea, in particular, always draws me close to God. I love the sound of the waves on the shore, and the expanse and distant horizon speaks to me of God's power and majesty. I also find my annual silent retreat really helps me meet with God.

What is your favourite way to spend your day off?

A lie in, a spot of gardening, time with family or friends in the countryside, or watching a film or play would be perfect!

Recommended reading

'Where can wisdom be found?' (Job 24:12)

Is Your God Too Small? faces that question head on. Job struggled with huge questions about suffering – his own and the world's. He looked for an answer in the past, but discovered that it lay elsewhere, in God and in the divine presence. This accessible book opens Job for today's church, encouraging us to enlarge our view of God and his goodness in difficult times, making it a must-read in the context of the world's problems today.

The following is an extract from the Epilogue of the book.

Popular religion has shaped its god into someone who is warm and comfortable, who is kind and gentle, who can be relied upon to be nice to us. This is the deity that New Atheism mocks and rejects. How can such a god exist who allows so much suffering in the world he claims to have made? It is a fair jibe! It is belief in such a God that prompts our complaint that it is unfair when life serves up suffering and war and disease and death.

If Job's struggle teaches us anything, it teaches us that God is not 'nice'. There is a bigness about God that dwarfs us – dwarfs our virtue, our understanding, our theology. We do not have enough words in our vocabulary to describe him. His holiness is beyond our purest thoughts, his knowledge more comprehensive than the most encyclopedic libraries can embrace, his wisdom beyond what the most profound philosophy can begin to deduce, his eternity simply unimaginable to time-bound thought.

How then are we to understand ourselves, our circumstances, our times? We want to understand; we need to understand, for we are creatures hardwired to expect life to have meaning. We live in a rational universe that functions according to largely predictable forces and patterns. But when life takes a turn we do not expect, we want to know why. We too would like to be able to scale down the immensity of God in order to put our questions and find out what is going on and why. Not surprisingly, many who turn to the book of Job do so hoping to find an answer to the problem of suffering. Surely here, in the story of one man's legendary experience of unrelenting pain, we can find a way of responding to that lifelong question: Why? So what can we say with certainty?

First, there are no easy answers! For Job's friends, there was one obvious explanation that, had Job been more honest with himself (in their view), he would have accepted. They were wrong. The reason for Job's suffering remained out of reach to them and to Job. They would never have come close to finding it even if they had debated for years.

Second, suffering cannot be explained as simply as drawing a straight line between sin and punishment. Granted, the Bible does make that link from time to time, both generally and in specific instances. Clearly the world would be a different place if sin had not entered. We see that in the consequences of Adam and Eve's sin (Genesis 3:14–19), and in the enormous contrast with the new heaven and earth (Revelation 21:1–8). God warned his people that disobedience would give physical and natural consequences like famine and exile (e.g. Deuteronomy 28). Paul mentions that some Christians in Corinth were ill because they had abused the Lord's Supper (1 Corinthians 11:30), and James hints at the possibility of a link between sin and sickness in some cases (James 5:15). But to argue, as Job's friends did, that sickness is invariably punishment for sin is a serious mistake.

Third, Satan – or 'the Satan' as the book of Job describes the devil, intending to focus attention on his role as an adversary rather than his personhood – is limited in his power. He may accuse but is not at liberty to harm God's children except the Father permits it. We do not need to fear him if we remain close to God. In his classic tale, *Pilgrim's Progress*, John Bunyan imagines the devil as a lion on Christian's path, but he is chained! At the same time, we would be foolish to dismiss him as a figure of fun dressed in a red leotard carrying a three-pronged fork.

Fourth, if the book of Job has anything to teach us about suffering, it is not so much an explanation we need, but an experience of God himself, to learn the fear of God that gives wisdom. Disturbing that may be, but nothing will be more fulfilling, more likely to bring us peace. This was certainly the case for Job and can be for us, which is why I suggested that the book of Job is more about God than the human experience of tragedy and pain. What we learn from God here may seriously challenge what we have always believed about him.

When Job stood among the ruins of his family and his business and felt disease spreading across his body, he reached out to comfort his distraught wife as he prepared to become an exile from her and the community. Gently, he posed the question that rings in our ears as we read page after page of poetic discussion:

Shall we accept good from God, and not trouble?
JOB 2:10

It is not so much a question as an affirmation, for the answer implied must be, 'Yes, of course we will!' But is it something we too can affirm – you and me? That is the question that remains for us to answer.

If we also say 'Yes', we thereby affirm our willingness to accept whatever God sends into our lives. That is an enormous step of trust in his loving purpose for us and those dear to us, for it is possible that God will take us along a path not unlike the one Job had to walk. We had better understand the implications.

God's purpose for his world is comprehensive and immense beyond our capacity to understand. So that Job could grasp this, God took him on a virtual tour of the universe. He brought into view its diversity and mystery, its tiny detail and its complexity. Job was shown constellations as well as the ostrich egg laying exposed on the desert floor. He was reminded of the strength of the crocodile as well as the shimmering beauty of its scales. With every fresh glimpse of the world around him, Job grew a little smaller and saw God as even greater. It would do us good to switch off our phones and tablets and TVs and step outside more often to experience the same change of perspective.

As we look into God's revelation of himself in the Bible, we learn that God is at work in the world fulfilling his purpose – and that purpose is all-encompassing. Paul begins his letter to Christians in Ephesus with a discussion on predestination – what a way to start a letter! If we leap over the verses argued about for centuries, we get to the heart of his amazing insight:

[God] works out everything in conformity with the purpose of his will.
EPHESIANS 1:11

Note this: God's purpose embraces 'everything' and he ensures that it does what he wants! What God determines, God does. We could start up the age-old debate about God's sovereignty and human responsibility, but it is unlikely that we will ever explain the relationship between the two. We end up giving greater importance to one or the other for different reasons. The fact is that this is a mystery and, if God had actually given a clear explanation, we would still be no wiser because it lies outside categories with which we are familiar. We are too finite, too limited to understand the 'everything', let alone how it can be made to function 'in conformity with the purpose of his will'.

To order a copy of this book, please use the order form on page 149.

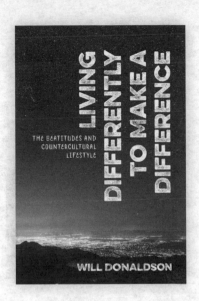

This book is for those who want to make a difference, to change the world one step at a time. Jesus Christ calls us in the beatitudes to live an authentic, countercultural lifestyle. By being different we can make a difference, becoming the salt of the earth and the light of the world. Through living the beatitudes, we could reflect the beauty of God's grace, grow in our likeness to Jesus and make the world a better place.

Living Differently to Make a Difference
The beatitudes and countercultural lifestyle
Will Donaldson
pb, 978 0 85746 671 6 £7.99
brfonline.org.uk

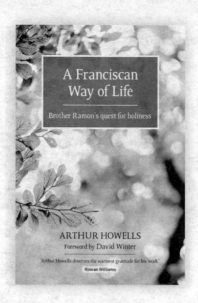

Be inspired by one man's unflinching faith in God.

Brother Ramon was a much-loved writer and speaker who died in 2000 – a man who delighted in life and people, and who chose solitude to practise the presence of God. This first biography, written by his friend, has warmth and spiritual insight. It tells of his life's pilgrimage; his quest for holiness as a Franciscan friar; his inner journey of discovery and transformation; his love of God; and his influence on others. The selection from his writings which concludes the book illustrates his spiritual journey. This book will be an inspiration to readers to live lives fully for Jesus Christ.

A Franciscan Way of Life
Brother Ramon's quest for holiness
Arthur Howells
pb, 978 0 85746 662 4 £8.99
brfonline.org.uk

To order

Online: **brfonline.org.uk**
Telephone: +44 (0)1865 319700
Mon–Fri 9.15–17.30

Delivery times within the UK are normally
15 working days. Prices are correct at the time of
going to press but may change without prior notice.

Title	Price	Qty	Total
Anxious Times	£3.99		
What Would Jesus Post?	£7.99		
Is Your God Too Small?	£7.99		
Living Differently to Make a Difference	£7.99		
A Franciscan Way of Life	£8.99		

POSTAGE AND PACKING CHARGES			
Order value	UK	Europe	Rest of world
Under £7.00	£2.00	£5.00	£7.00
£7.00–£29.99	£3.00	£9.00	£15.00
£30.00 and over	FREE	£9.00 + 15% of order value	£15.00 + 20% of order value

Total value of books	
Postage and packing	
Total for this order	

Please complete in BLOCK CAPITALS

Title .... First name/initials .... Surname ....

Address ....

.... Postcode ....

Acc. No. .... Telephone ....

Email ....

Method of payment

❏ Cheque (made payable to BRF) ❏ MasterCard / Visa

Card no. ⬚⬚⬚⬚ ⬚⬚⬚⬚ ⬚⬚⬚⬚ ⬚⬚⬚⬚ ⬚⬚⬚⬚

Valid from M M Y Y Expires M M Y Y Security code* ⬚⬚⬚

Last 3 digits on the reverse of the card

Signature* .... Date .... / .... / ....

*ESSENTIAL IN ORDER TO PROCESS YOUR ORDER

Please return this form to: BRF, 15 The Chambers, Vineyard, Abingdon OX14 3FE | enquiries@brf.org.uk
To read our terms and find out about cancelling your order, please visit **brfonline.org.uk/terms**.

The Bible Reading Fellowship (BRF) is a Registered Charity (233280)

How to encourage Bible reading in your church

BRF has been helping individuals connect with the Bible for over 90 years. We want to support churches as they seek to encourage church members into regular Bible reading.

Order a Bible reading resources pack

This pack is designed to give your church the tools to publicise our Bible reading notes. It includes:

- Sample Bible reading notes for your congregation to try.
- Publicity resources, including a poster.
- A church magazine feature about Bible reading notes.

The pack is free, but we welcome a £5 donation to cover the cost of postage. If you require a pack to be sent outside the UK or require a specific number of sample Bible reading notes, please contact us for postage costs. More information about what the current pack contains is available on our website.

How to order and find out more

- Visit **biblereadingnotes.org.uk/for-churches**
- Telephone BRF on +44 (0)1865 319700 Mon–Fri 9.15–17.30
- Write to us at BRF, 15 The Chambers, Vineyard, Abingdon OX14 3FE

Keep informed about our latest initiatives

We are continuing to develop resources to help churches encourage people into regular Bible reading, wherever they are on their journey. Join our email list at **biblereadingnotes.org.uk/helpingchurches** to stay informed about the latest initiatives that your church could benefit from.

Introduce a friend to our notes

We can send information about our notes and current prices for you to pass on. Please contact us.

Transforming lives and communities

BRF is a charity that is passionate about making a difference through the Christian faith. We want to see lives and communities transformed through our creative programmes and resources for individuals, churches and schools. We are doing this by resourcing:

- **Christian growth and understanding of the Bible.** Through our Bible reading notes, books, digital resources, Quiet Days and other events, we're resourcing individuals, groups and leaders in churches for their own spiritual journey and for their ministry.
- **Church outreach in the local community.** BRF is the home of three programmes that churches are embracing to great effect as they seek to engage with their local communities: Messy Church, Who Let The Dads Out? and The Gift of Years.
- **Teaching Christianity in primary schools.** Our Barnabas in Schools team is working with primary-aged children and their teachers, enabling them to explore Christianity creatively and confidently within the school curriculum.
- **Children's and family ministry.** Through our Parenting for Faith programme, websites and published resources, we're working with churches and families, enabling children and adults alike to explore Christianity creatively and bring the Bible alive.

Do you share our vision?

Sales of our books and Bible reading notes cover the cost of producing them. However, our other programmes are funded primarily by donations, grants and legacies. If you share our vision, would you help us to transform even more lives and communities? Your prayers and financial support are vital for the work that we do.

- You could support BRF's ministry with a one-off gift or regular donation (using the response form on page 153).
- You could consider making a bequest to BRF in your will (page 152).
- You could encourage your church to support BRF as part of your church's giving to home mission – perhaps focusing on a specific area of our ministry, or a particular member of our Barnabas in Schools team.
- Most important of all, you could support BRF with your prayers.

Creating character through gifts in wills

Across England, and in many parts of the world, children are beginning school after the summer holidays. Some will start studying new subjects this year or will be preparing for important exams; others will be going to school for the first time with equal levels of excitement and trepidation.

Our school years are an important time of growth and preparation. We learn all sorts of things, from the square root of 56 to the date of the start of World War II (in case you're wondering, the answers are 7.48 and 1 September 1939). Yet it's often the soft skills that we develop that we continue to draw on throughout our lives. Things such as how to work effectively with other people or deal with conflict and disappointment.

At BRF we're passionate about transforming lives and communities through the Christian faith. One of the ways to do this is by teaching about Christian values and the Bible through Barnabas RE Days. These explore values such as friendship, community and resilience; and ask questions like 'what is character?' and 'how does it form the people that we are and the communities we belong to?'

Around 23,200 children experienced our Barnabas RE Days and related events last year, and over 25,500 ideas for classroom studies and assemblies were downloaded from our website. Much of this work is only possible because of the generosity of those that support us during their lifetime and through gifts in wills.

Gifts in wills are an important source of income for us and they don't need to be huge to make a real difference. Will you help us transform more lives and communities through a gift in your will?

 For further information about making a gift to BRF in your will, please visit **brf.org.uk/lastingdifference**, contact Sophie Aldred on **+44 (0)1865 319700** or email **giving@brf.org.uk**.

Whatever you can do or give, we thank you for your support.

SHARING OUR VISION – MAKING A GIFT

I would like to make a gift to support BRF. Please use my gift for:

☐ where it is needed most ☐ Barnabas in Schools ☐ Parenting for Faith
☐ Messy Church ☐ Who Let The Dads Out? ☐ The Gift of Years

Title	First name/initials	Surname	
Address			
			Postcode
Email			
Telephone			
Signature			Date

giftaid it You can add an extra 25p to every £1 you give.

Please treat as Gift Aid donations all qualifying gifts of money made

☐ today, ☐ in the past four years, ☐ and in the future.

I am a UK taxpayer and understand that if I pay less Income Tax and/or Capital Gains Tax in the current tax year than the amount of Gift Aid claimed on all my donations, it is my responsibility to pay any difference.

☐ My donation does not qualify for Gift Aid.

Please notify BRF if you want to cancel this Gift Aid declaration, change your name or home address, or no longer pay sufficient tax on your income and/or capital gains.

Please complete other side of form ➲

Please return this form to:
BRF, 15 The Chambers, Vineyard, Abingdon OX14 3FE

The Bible Reading Fellowship is a Registered Charity (233280)

SHARING OUR VISION – MAKING A GIFT

Regular giving

By Direct Debit:

☐ I would like to make a regular gift of £ ⬚⬚⬚⬚ per month/quarter/year.
Please also complete the Direct Debit instruction on page 159.

By Standing Order:

Please contact Priscilla Kew +44 (0)1235 462305 | giving@brf.org.uk

One-off donation

Please accept my gift of:

☐ £10 ☐ £50 ☐ £100 Other £ ⬚⬚⬚⬚

by (delete as appropriate):

☐ Cheque/Charity Voucher payable to 'BRF'

☐ MasterCard/Visa/Debit card/Charity card

Name on card

Card no. ☐☐☐☐ ☐☐☐☐ ☐☐☐☐ ☐☐☐☐

Valid from M M Y Y Expires M M Y Y

Security code* ☐☐☐ *Last 3 digits on the reverse of the card
ESSENTIAL IN ORDER TO PROCESS YOUR PAYMENT

Signature   Date

We like to acknowledge all donations. However, if you do not wish to receive an acknowledgement, please tick here ☐

↻ Please complete other side of form

Please return this form to:
BRF, 15 The Chambers, Vineyard, Abingdon OX14 3FE

ND0318

NEW DAYLIGHT SUBSCRIPTION RATES

Please note our new subscription rates, current until 30 April 2019:

Individual subscriptions
covering 3 issues for under 5 copies, payable in advance
(including postage & packing):

	UK	Europe	Rest of world
New Daylight	£16.95	£25.20	£29.10
New Daylight 3-year subscription (9 issues) (not available for Deluxe)	£46.35	N/A	N/A
New Daylight Deluxe per set of 3 issues p.a.	£21.45	£32.25	£38.25

Group subscriptions
covering 3 issues for 5 copies or more, sent to **one** UK address (post free):

New Daylight	£13.50 per set of 3 issues p.a.
New Daylight Deluxe	£17.25 per set of 3 issues p.a.

Please note that the annual billing period for group subscriptions runs from 1 May to 30 April.

Overseas group subscription rates
Available on request. Please email **enquiries@brf.org.uk**.

Copies may also be obtained from Christian bookshops:

New Daylight	£4.50 per copy
New Daylight Deluxe	£5.75 per copy

All our Bible reading notes can be ordered online by visiting
biblereadingnotes.org.uk/subscriptions

For information about our other Bible reading notes,
and apps for iPhone and iPod touch, visit
biblereadingnotes.org.uk

NEW DAYLIGHT INDIVIDUAL SUBSCRIPTION FORM

All our Bible reading notes can be ordered online by visiting
biblereadingnotes.org.uk/subscriptions

☐ I would like to take out a subscription:

Title .... First name/initials .... Surname ....

Address ....

.... Postcode ....

Telephone .... Email ....

Please send *New Daylight* beginning with the January 2019 / May 2019 / September 2019 issue (*delete as appropriate*):

(please tick box)

	UK	Europe	Rest of world
New Daylight 1-year subscription	☐ £16.95	☐ £25.20	☐ £29.10
New Daylight 3-year subscription	☐ £46.35	N/A	N/A
New Daylight Deluxe	☐ £21.45	☐ £32.25	☐ £38.25

Total enclosed £ .... (cheques should be made payable to 'BRF')

Please charge my MasterCard / Visa ☐ Debit card ☐ with £ ....

Card no. ☐☐☐☐ ☐☐☐☐ ☐☐☐☐ ☐☐☐☐

Valid from ☐☐ ☐☐ Expires ☐☐ ☐☐ Security code* ☐☐☐

Last 3 digits on the reverse of the card

Signature* .... Date .... /....... /.......

*ESSENTIAL IN ORDER TO PROCESS YOUR PAYMENT

To set up a Direct Debit, please also complete the Direct Debit instruction on page 159 and return it to BRF with this form.

Please return this form with the appropriate payment to:
BRF, 15 The Chambers, Vineyard, Abingdon OX14 3FE

To read our terms and find out about cancelling your order, please visit **brfonline.org.uk/terms**.

The Bible Reading Fellowship is a Registered Charity (233280)

ND0318

NEW DAYLIGHT GIFT SUBSCRIPTION FORM

☐ I would like to give a gift subscription (please provide both names and addresses):

Title .... First name/initials .... Surname ....

Address ....

.... Postcode ....

Telephone .... Email ....

Gift subscription name ....

Gift subscription address ....

.... Postcode ....

Gift message (20 words max. or include your own gift card):

....

....

Please send *New Daylight* beginning with the January 2019 / May 2019 / September 2019 issue (*delete as appropriate*):

(*please tick box*)	UK	Europe	Rest of world
New Daylight 1-year subscription	☐ £16.95	☐ £25.20	☐ £29.10
New Daylight 3-year subscription	☐ £46.35	N/A	N/A
New Daylight Deluxe	☐ £21.45	☐ £32.25	☐ £38.25

Total enclosed £ .... (cheques should be made payable to 'BRF')

Please charge my MasterCard / Visa ☐ Debit card ☐ with £ ....

Card no. ☐☐☐☐ ☐☐☐☐ ☐☐☐☐ ☐☐☐☐

Valid from ☐☐ ☐☐ Expires ☐☐ ☐☐ Security code* ☐☐☐

Last 3 digits on the reverse of the card

Signature* .... Date ....../....../......

*ESSENTIAL IN ORDER TO PROCESS YOUR PAYMENT

To set up a Direct Debit, please also complete the Direct Debit instruction on page 159 and return it to BRF with this form.

Please return this form with the appropriate payment to:
BRF, 15 The Chambers, Vineyard, Abingdon OX14 3FE

To read our terms and find out about cancelling your order, please visit **brfonline.org.uk/terms**.

The Bible Reading Fellowship is a Registered Charity (233280)

DIRECT DEBIT PAYMENT

You can pay for your annual subscription to our Bible reading notes using Direct Debit. You need only give your bank details once, and the payment is made automatically every year until you cancel it. If you would like to pay by Direct Debit, please use the form opposite, entering your BRF account number under 'Reference number'.

You are fully covered by the Direct Debit Guarantee:

The Direct Debit Guarantee

- This Guarantee is offered by all banks and building societies that accept instructions to pay Direct Debits.

- If there are any changes to the amount, date or frequency of your Direct Debit, The Bible Reading Fellowship will notify you 10 working days in advance of your account being debited or as otherwise agreed. If you request The Bible Reading Fellowship to collect a payment, confirmation of the amount and date will be given to you at the time of the request.

- If an error is made in the payment of your Direct Debit, by The Bible Reading Fellowship or your bank or building society, you are entitled to a full and immediate refund of the amount paid from your bank or building society.

- If you receive a refund you are not entitled to, you must pay it back when The Bible Reading Fellowship asks you to.

- You can cancel a Direct Debit at any time by simply contacting your bank or building society. Written confirmation may be required. Please also notify us.

The Bible Reading Fellowship

Instruction to your bank or building society to pay by Direct Debit

Please fill in the whole form using a ballpoint pen and return it to:
BRF, 15 The Chambers, Vineyard, Abingdon OX14 3FE

Service User Number: | 5 | 5 | 8 | 2 | 2 | 9 |

Name and full postal address of your bank or building society

To: The Manager	Bank/Building Society
Address	
	Postcode

Name(s) of account holder(s)

Branch sort code

| | | – | | | – | | |

Bank/Building Society account number

| | | | | | | | | |

Reference number

| | | | | | | | |

Instruction to your Bank/Building Society
Please pay The Bible Reading Fellowship Direct Debits from the account detailed in this instruction, subject to the safeguards assured by the Direct Debit Guarantee. I understand that this instruction may remain with The Bible Reading Fellowship and, if so, details will be passed electronically to my bank/building society.

Signature(s)

Banks and Building Societies may not accept Direct Debit instructions for some types of account.

Transforming
lives and communities

Christian growth and understanding of the Bible

Resourcing individuals, groups and leaders in churches for their own spiritual journey and for their ministry

Church outreach in the local community

Offering three programmes that churches are embracing to great effect as they seek to engage with their local communities and transform lives

Teaching Christianity in primary schools

Working with children and teachers to explore Christianity creatively and confidently

Children's and family ministry

Working with churches and families to explore Christianity creatively and bring the Bible alive

Visit **brf.org.uk** for more information on BRF's work

brf.org.uk